EXPLORING
SOLWAY
HISTORY

EXPLORING
SOLWAY
HISTORY

PHILIP NIXON ARPS. LMPA. DipPP

AND

HUGH DIAS

breedon **books**
PUBLISHING

First published in Great Britain in 2007 by

The Breedon Books Publishing Company Limited

Breedon House, 3 The Parker Centre, Derby, DE21 4SZ.

Acknowledgements

In appreciation of their excellent help and support the authors would like to thank:

Val Nixon, Sophy Nixon, Mark Nixon, John Humphries, John Stephenson, Jim Hawkins, Joe Dias, Tom Dias and Denis Dunlop.

The Dean and Chapter of Carlisle Cathedral, Ian Power of Carlisle Castle, English Heritage, Tullie House Museum.

And Steve Caron, Michelle Grainger and Matt Limbert of Breedon Books.

ISBN 978-1-85983-586-9

Printed and bound by Butler and Tanner, Frome, Somerset.

Contents

Solway Firth near Gretna.

Introduction

Solway Firth looking towards Port Carlisle in early morning, English side.

Most people roar past it on the M6, heading north for the Highlands or south to the Lake District, ignoring one of the secret gems of Britain. The Solway Firth and its adjacent coastlines on both sides of the border are still mainly undiscovered and unspoilt by the tourist trade and have an ability to cast a spell on anyone sensitive to history and beauty.

It has a subtle, haunting charm. On the Scottish side the majestic Criffel frames huge expanses of sand and mudflats reflecting the colours of spectacular sunsets, and haaf netters still fish for salmon like their Viking ancestors. On the English side the plain rises gently to meet Skiddaw and Blencathra, watching over the scene like giant sentinels. Lying in between is the silver ribbon of the Solway.

Solway Firth – Airds Point with Criffel in the distance, Scottish side.

Solway Coast near Scar Point, Scottish side.

The interplay of light, sand and water guarantees constant movement, atmosphere and colour, and in winter the sounds of thousands of wild geese, curlews, plovers and oyster catchers can have a strange pull on the wild, atavistic strain in the imagination.

From a distance the canvas is breathtaking, but the splendour is laced with danger. The tides that ebb and flow twice a day sweep in at a running pace and over the years they have claimed many lives. The river channels of the Esk, Nith and Eden are constantly moving and quicksands will appear overnight in unexpected places. The advice we were given as children when holidaying at Port Carlisle was always to keep running if the feet were beginning to sink. We heard the story of one marshland farmer who left his tractor within touching distance of the sands overnight and the next morning it had all but disappeared, the only visible sign of it being the cabin roof. The warning should be repeated again and again: there is a terrible beauty in the Solway, and wandering too far from the shore is a very risky business indeed unless you know the tide times and the river channels.

The landscape itself is breathtaking enough and as a child I was mesmerised by the daily discoveries outside the cottage door. A few fields away was the peat moss, where a man had once killed 40 adders on a morning's walk. Coming towards me was grinning Uncle Ronnie holding up a salmon, sparkling silver in the sunlight, almost as big as myself. You could tread for flounders in the tidal pools, feeling for the squirm and grabbing

Looking across the salt flats to Criffel, Scottish side.

*The view from
Herdhill Scar
towards
Cardurnock,
English side.*

them if you were quick enough. There was Fell's farm, where you could make dens in the hay and swing from the rope on the ledge and soar on to the bales 20ft below. There were dams to be made in the streams, blackberry picking competitions and potatoes to be roasted on our own fires, making sure that nearby gorse bushes didn't explode into flames from one of the sparks.

These are childish memories, always to be cherished as they capture moments when life was in complete harmony and every morning was a new adventure. They are magical enough, but there is another dimension to the Solway that was only realised in later years when an interest in its history began to form.

Down this lane the dying Edward I, the Hammer of the Scots, was dragged on his litter to face his old enemy across the Firth; on the moss outside the cottage King John had come to regain his health. Across this ford or wath Prince Charlie and his Highlanders had waded into England; Reiver bands had splashed their way across the channels with stolen herds of cattle. On the Watch Hill near Burgh by Sands, the native Brigantes had spied on Roman galleys nosing up the River Eden. Nearby Bowness was built on the foundations of the second biggest camp on the Roman wall; and flickering tantalisingly in the background were the controversial shadows of Merlin and Arthur.

It began to dawn on me that although the English side of the Solway is now designated as an area of outstanding natural beauty, it has also been an area of outstanding natural violence.

This was once one of the most dangerous frontiers in Europe, subject to invasion, raid, counter raid, general lawlessness and havoc. As a buffer zone between two aggressive nations, the dogs of war ran freely and viciously all over it and for a time it was practically ungovernable. Sheep may now safely graze on the marshes, but during the Reiver times most people from Dumfries to

Berwick could rarely sleep easily in their beds, and no cattle or beast could be left unguarded for long. Not only was the Solway a regular invasion route for 1,500 years, but it was also the western flank of the infamous Border Reiver country in the 15th and 16th century.

It would really require separate volumes to tell the tale for each period and this book has no pretensions at giving the complete picture, or even of scholarly research. Most of the detail is already well known and we hope that it might only help the visitor or interested local to peer a little more searchingly into the apparent blandness of the view around them.

Today the Solway on both the Scottish and English sides wears its history modestly. It doesn't shout at the tourist or lay extravagant claims. 'Take a look if you want,' it seems to say, and judge for yourself.

I hope that we haven't offended anyone

west of Castle Douglas and south of Maryport who would consider themselves as worthy of inclusion in a book on the Solway. We had to stop somewhere…

Finally, if anyone has read this far it will become obvious that, having had strong roots on the English side of the Solway there may be a touch of bias in the telling. Far from it. To me the border is arbitrary and hardly noticed and I am as enchanted as anyone that such giants as Sir Walter Scott and Robbie Burns felt welcome across the water. This, a region that once had Carlisle as the capital of Scotland and was part of the ancient kingdom of Strathclyde, was united in its fight against the encroaching Saxons from the east and the Picts from the north. The Solway wasn't a barrier; it was an ancient trade route that linked the region together and it was significant that the Reivers took not the slightest notice when a 'border' was drawn. It is an extraordinary story.

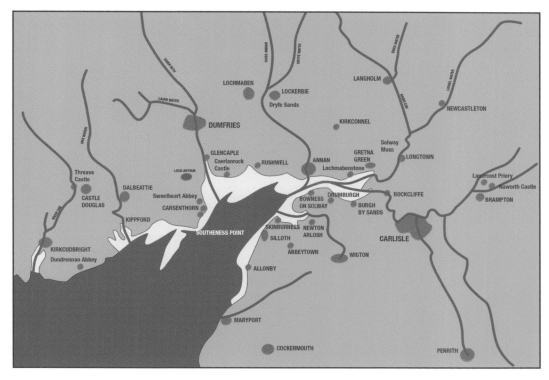

The road bridge, Allonby, Cumbria.

The English Side of the Solway

ALLONBY

Allonby, Cumbria — houses on the coastal flats.

Allonby was once a popular 19th-century holiday resort and today, with its sand dunes, tiny river, bridge and colourful cottages, it is still a place of great charm. In the main street there is an impressive colonnaded building which was once an indoor baths for Victorians, who liked their sea water warmed up before they immersed themselves. It is not known where the village gets its name from, but one theory is that it was named after Alan, son of Waldeve and the second Lord of Allerdale. He had just undertaken to restore the Abbey of Holme and, being of a solitary and retiring nature, he liked the peace and quiet of the place and chose it as his home, hence the name 'Alan's bay'.

One of its most famous visitors was Charles Dickens, who came here in 1857 with his literary companion Wilkie Collins. Collins was laid up at the Ship Inn nursing an ankle which he had sprained on a walk and, perhaps in a bad humour, Dickens made some disparaging remarks about the place in his story *The Lazy Tour of Two Idle Apprentices*. He did add, though, that he was very impressed by the spectacular sunsets and the view over the Solway to Criffel. The village

Victorian Houses, Allonby.

also appears in the novel *Guy Mannering* by Sir Walter Scott, where there is mention of the old smuggling days at the tidal harbour and further down at the Saltpans.

Allonby Bay was the scene of a dramatic shipwreck in February 1903. The *Hougomont*, a sailing vessel with 32 passengers on board, had sailed from San Francisco and had reached the mouth of the River Mersey when a ferocious storm forced it up to the Solway as far as Maryport. A Liverpool tug followed her up and took her in tow, but the ship had to slip cable and was driven further north into Allonby Bay, where the huge waves began to break her up.

Everyone was eventually rescued, but the captain, who had been a master for 32 years and had sailed all over the world, said he had never spent such a terrifying night in his life.

ARTHURET

This tiny hamlet half a mile to the south of Longtown could possibly have been one of the most dramatic places on the Border. The earliest church here may have been founded by St Kentigern in the sixth century, but the earliest connections are with Jedburgh Abbey in 1150.

The present church, dedicated to St Michael and all Angels, was built in 1609 after the union of the crowns of England and Scotland. King James I was disturbed to hear that the local people were without a faith and the building was financed through a national subscription.

The bluff on which the church stands overlooks the scene of numerous tragedies. In 1542 the battle of Solway Moss was fought

St Michael and All Angels Church, Arthuret, Cumbria.

two miles away. This was a disaster for the Scots, whose king, James V, died of a broken heart soon afterwards. In December 1771 the bogland near here was so saturated by torrential rain that it erupted, covering the surrounding fields and houses in a 30ft thick layer of peat.

But it is much further back in time that the real significance of Arthuret lies. Arthurian scholars, such as the late Norma Goodrich, claim that the last of King Arthur's 12 battles Camboglanna (Camlann) was fought a few miles to the east and that his body was brought here after he was wounded and then transported to an embarkation point on the Solway. In those days the Esk was navigable up to Netherby and Roman moorings have

Solway Moss from Arthuret Church Yard.

The Well, Arthuret.

Arthuret Knowes.

doubt is that one of the most crucial battles in British history was fought here in 573, when an early Christian King, Rhydderch, defeated a pagan army from the north. Legend has it that the carnage was so appalling that a descendant of Arthur, or Merlin, fled the scene to the Forest of Celidon in southern Scotland and eventually went mad.

Near the church on the west side and situated halfway down the escarpment is a spring known as St Michael's Well, and it is believed that St Kentigern first preached the Christian faith here in the mid-sixth century before he settled at Hoddom. There is also a legend that he met the insane Merlin after the battle of Ardderyd and gave him the Blessed Sacrament here.

The church itself is situated on a raised platform above the flood plain of the River Esk. Just behind it and across the road are two small little hills called the Arthuret Knowes. The top of the highest was fortified by a small earthen rampart. Whatever its function, it would have been a superb defensive and observation site overlooking the vast Solway

been found there. She also suggests that Arthuret could be a corruption of 'Arthur's head'.

This is quite a claim, but it does have some historical backing. In 1668 Dr Hugh Todd, a rector of Arthuret, started a parish register ,and among the notes in his own handwriting is one stating that 'Arhturritt or Arthurrid has its name from the famous King Arthur, King of the ancient Britons, in whose time there was a battle fought here, probably on the moor called by that name.' The claim is that Arthur died in around 542, but what is not in

plain and guarding the northern approaches to Carlisle.

Archie Armstrong

He was the official court jester to King James I and his son Charles, and he is buried next to an ancient mediaeval cross in the churchyard. Another role he had was that of gentleman groom of the chambers, and he would travel ahead of the king on journeys to make sure that everything was in order for the royal visit. James must have had a soft spot for him because he granted Archie a patent for the manufacture of tobacco pipes, even though he hated the stuff himself. He must have been a bit of a man on the make because he would also annoy his master by presenting petitions to him for a fee from the petitioners…

He went too far, though, with his jibe against the Archbishop of Canterbury, William Laud. Archie was asked to say grace at an official dinner and he said

'Give great praise to God and little laud to the devil…' The king had no option but to sack him and Archie was banished from the court.

The ancient cross mentioned above is thought to be Maltese, possibly erected by one of the Knights of Malta in the 14th or 15th century.

BOWNESS ON SOLWAY

This was the site of the second largest fort on the Wall called 'Maia'. The village is built almost entirely on top of it and one day excavations might reveal a staggering number of artefacts. Scotland is only a mile away

Archie Armstrong's grave is traditionally thought to be near the Maltese Cross in Arthuret Churchyard.

The village of Bowness is built on the site of a Roman Fort.

The main street of the attractive village of Bowness on Solway...

across the Solway and this was the reason for the fort being built here. It is the last fordable spot on the Solway and was of significant strategic importance. The name 'Bowness', written in earlier days 'Bulness', indicates a bulge or swelling, a rounded headland.

The fort defences were originally a turf rampart with timber gates, but these were replaced with stone in the second century AD. The field opposite the Wallsend Guest House has many ridges and bumps, which contain the remains of many buildings. The problem involved in excavation is that the sandstone would rapidly decay if exposed to the air.

There was much raiding and counter-raiding in the reiving days and in the porch of

...has many architecturally interesting buildings.

the Church of the Archangel Michael are two old bells marked 1611 and 1616. They tell a remarkable story. According to legend, two Scotsmen crossed the Solway in a boat and stole the bells from the church. They were chased across the sands and, to lighten their boat, they threw the bells into the water. In retaliation Bowness men paid a similar visit to Scotland, stealing two bells from churches in Dornock and Middlebie. According to tradition, for hundreds of years every new vicar of Annan Church has written to the vicar of Bowness church asking for their return. Apparently the requests are politely refused. One of the channels of the River Esk opposite Dornock is still called the Bell Pool today.

Another story is about a man called Aeneas Sylvius, who later became Pope Pius II. He arrived in Bowness in 1435 on a papal mission to contact King Edward I, who was over the Solway in Sweetheart Abbey warring against the Scots. The whole village turned out to see him eat with the local priest, although they soon disappeared 'to flee to a tower a long way off for fear of Scots who were wont to pass over at ebb of tide'. During the night geese and dogs raised the alarm and Sylvius's guides and attendants deserted him in panic. Apparently the whole thing was a hoax to get rid of an unwelcome visitor.

A more poignant story concerns the wife of a Scottish smuggler who was drowned on a free trading run to England. In 1775 Thomas Stowell was aboard a boat smuggling brandy and tobacco when it was challenged by one of the king's boats from Skinburness. They were chased into the Bowness channel and shots were fired. Young Thomas was killed and in the churchyard a headstone of Snaefell slate beneath a yew tree marks his grave. It is reported that the widow had the stone brought over by boat and carried it to the churchyard herself.

Beneath the same yew tree are the unmarked graves of six other smugglers from the Isle of Man who were drowned in the Solway in 1762.

Carving of what is believed to be a Celtic head in St Michael's Church

In 2007 Bowness is undergoing something of a mini revival with the recent opening of the Roman Wall Path National Trail finishing on the restored 'Banks' overlooking the Firth. To the west of the village is the RSPB Campfield Nature Reserve. The saltmarshes support some of the largest wader roosts on the Solway. At high tide there are thousands of oystercatchers, curlews, bar-tailed godwits, dunlin, knot, redshanks and grey plovers to be seen. It is also home to huge numbers of barnacle and pink-footed geese during the winter months.

St Michael's Church, Burgh by Sands.

*Statue of Edward I
– Burgth by Sands.*

BURGH BY SANDS

Pronounced 'Bruff', this is a village of mainly 17th and 18th-century houses and it stands near the remains of a Roman fort built in around AD95. It was called 'Aballava', meaning orchard, and it included troops from Germany, Holland and North Africa. Later a larger one was built housing 500 cavalry, which would have been ready to cover any threat from the north very rapidly. The 13th-century castle is now demolished, but the two fields where it stood have a typical border ring to their names. They are called 'Spill-blood-holme' and 'Hangman-tree'…

The Barony of Burgh was created in 1092 as a defensive area against Scottish invasion from across the Solway. It was first granted to Norman barons such as the D'Estrivers, Engaines, Morvilles, Lucies, De Multons, Dacres and Howards before being sold in 1685 to Sir John Lowther. His descendants, the Earls of Lonsdale, still hold the title today.

The tiny Church of St Michael stands within the area of the fort at the east end of the village and it has a magnificent history.

Built in 1180 from stones from the nearby Roman wall, it is a classic example of a border pele tower at each end, one of which was to provide safety for the vicar, and at the foot of it grooves have been worked into the stone. They record the place where village men would sharpen their swords and spears before going on a raid.

The church was built to last, with small windows, seven and a half foot thick walls and a massive oak door protected with iron

*The Edward I
monument, Burgh
marsh.*

*Opposite: The nave
and chancel. St
Michael's Church,
Burgh by Sands.*

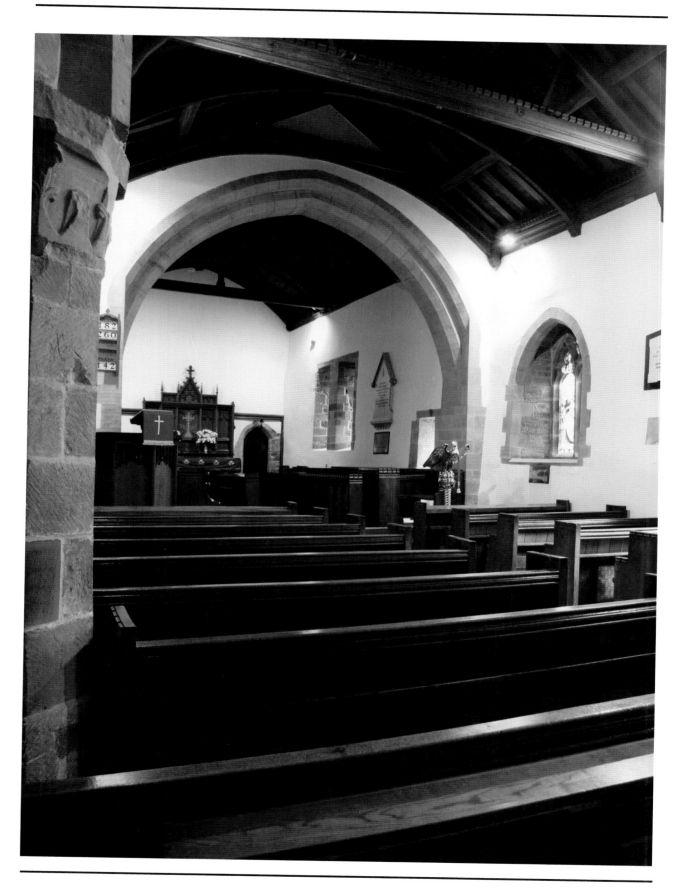

crosses. It didn't turn the other cheek. Above the door is a window designed to throw anything conveniently heavy or boiling out of onto attackers below. The church also had a tolerant attitude to blood sports: unll the beginning of the 19th century the village cockpit was located in its grounds…

In July 1307 the church was the focus of national mourning. King Edward I, the Hammer of the Scots, died on the nearby marshes and his body lay in state in the church for 11 days. It must have been an amazing spectacle, as hundreds of courtiers and the nobility of England paid their last respects in and around the tiny church.

This entire pageant would have been camped a mile to the north on the marshes near the Peatwath. It is now a wild and peaceful place, with a 19th-century monument to the dead king standing at a forlorn angle among the indifferent sheep. It replaced an earlier monument put up in 1685 by the Duke of Norfolk on the exact spot where he had had his royal tent.

Hogs back grave cover, St John's Church Crosscanonby.

Apart from being famous for its mushrooms, Burgh marsh was also a favourite place for horse racing, wrestling and athletic events. The barony Cup was first presented in 1690 and it was only raced for when there was a new Earl of Lonsdale. Throughout the 19th century there were five races and one of the cups is mentioned in Robert Anderson's ballad in 1804. 'The cup was aw siller, and letter'd reet neycely.' The last race was in April 1900.

Burgh was the home of a once famous but probably forgotten poet called John, or 'blin', Stagg, the fiddler. Born in 1770 he was the son of the village tailor, but was blinded by an accident and was forced to make a living by keeping a library at Wigton and playing the fiddle at wakes, weddings and other social gatherings.

He was a tall, good-looking man, much in demand, and by all accounts a lively, cheerful and witty character. In his day he was as famous as Robbie Burns and was popular with the local gentry. The Duke of Norfolk was always anxious for him to perform.

CROSSCANONBY

The name indicates that there was once a convent of canons here, possibly an outhouse of the Augustinian Canons at Carlisle, now the cathedral. What remains is a fine example of a Norman church dedicated to St John the Evangelist. It was built in about 1130 on a site where a Celtic missionary had set up a cross to mark his place of preaching. The church was developed in the 13th century, but it was

St John's Church, Crosscanonby.

not until a large restoration in 1880 that many ancient carved stones were discovered. These date mainly from the 10th and 11th century and include two large hog back stones, which are grave covers of pagan Anglo-Danish invaders, shaped like upturned boats. One is to be seen over the south doorway and the other in a corner outside the church.

Another interesting feature is the chancel arch, which is thought to have been the entrance to the commander's quarters at Maryport Roman fort. The Senhouse family who worshipped here before Maryport was built donated the stone to the church.

CROSSCANONBY SALT PANS

From Anglo-Saxon times salt production in Britain was almost as important an industry as agriculture and fishing, as it was the only preservative available. The Crosscanonby salt pans, built around 1650, are a fine example of a once-thriving industry.

The pans, owned mainly by various wealthy families and the monks of nearby Holme Cultram Abbey, were large, circular, elevated structures called sleech pits or kinches. These were made of cobbles with a clay-lined floor covered with reeds to act as a filter. Horse-drawn wagons would bring salt-laden sand from the shore and when this had been piled

The Saltpans, Crosscanonby.

Drumburgh
"Castle" dates from
1307.

into the pan, water was sprinkled over it. A strong salt solution would gather at the bottom and this was then gently boiled in iron pans. These were about nine feet by eight feet and up to eight feet deep.

The salt crystals were then collected in wicker baskets before being sold on. At one time the industry was so important that salt pans stretched from Silloth all the way south to Millom in a virtually unbroken line. They were always under threat from high Solway tides and in 1998 Solway Rural Initiative carried out major works at Crosscanonby to protect the pans from erosion, realising that major storm tides could destroy them forever.

DRUMBURGH

A few miles west of Burgh by Sands on a small clay knoll above the plain is Drumburgh (pronounced Drumbruff). The name is said to mean 'bog of the bitterns'. The Roman name for it is Congavata and it was recorded on an enamelled bronze vessel found in 2003. It is dominated by the old manor or castle house built in 1307 by Sir Richard le Brun. In Henry VIII's time it was fortified further by Lord Dacre, to guard the English end of the Sandwath, using stones from the nearby wall. The north side of the fort has been lost to the sea, but the castle is situated on the south side of the fort and is a prime example of a mediaeval defended house. Lord Dacre was an interesting character. He fought at the battle of Flodden, became Lord Warden of the English West March and stole his teenage bride from under the noses of her relations. Above the main door you can still see the Dacre coat of arms. In 1681 the castle passed into the ownership of Sir John Lowther and this date and his initials are on the door locks.

Walter Scott used it as 'Fairladies Mansion' in *Redgauntlet* and early editions of the *Waverley* novels used to contain an engraving of Drumburgh.

KIRKBRIDE

This small headland village was at one time almost entirely surrounded by the sea and a large Roman fort guarded one of their supply harbours there. There is a small 12th century church built mainly of Roman stones. According to legend the churchyard used to be visited by bodysnatchers who would carry their grim loads across the marsh to a waiting coach. The lane down from the church is known as the "Wine Lonnin" where contraband used to be bought to the old rectory (destroyed by fire in 1960) and three inns which have since become private houses.

LANERCOST PRIORY

Dedicated to St Mary Magdalene by Augustinian canons in 1169, the abbey has had a long and colourful history. Situated in the middle of a war zone, it faced bankruptcy from having to entertain the royal court or destruction from raids launched from Scotland by the Norman family of De Villibus, the Multons and later the Dacres. Strategically it was in the direct firing line of the Border

St Brides church, Kirkbride.

Edward I stayed at Lanercost Priory on his way to Burgh marsh.

conflict and was a prime target for Scottish raids for hundreds of years. When the English raided the religious houses of Kelso, Melrose, Dryburgh and Jedburgh, reprisals would swiftly follow. Stones to build and repair the abbey were taken from the nearby Roman Wall.

The abbot must have dreaded the arrival of Edward I, Queen Eleanor and the entire court in September 1306. This was the third time he had paid a visit, but by now he was an old man of 67 and this was his last attempt to subjugate Scotland. He was a dying man, probably suffering from dysentery, and he had to be carried into the abbey on a litter. He was on his way north to deal once and for all with what he saw as the rebellious Scots. Intending to stay for only a short while, his illness prevented him from moving and he stayed for six months. This put a huge strain on the resources of the abbey. It effectively became a small town and, in order to house the court, a huge wooden building, in effect a temporary palace, had to be built in the grounds.

The chronicles record interesting details of his stay. In the inner court alone there were over 200 people, including a personal bodyguard of seven Welshmen, two surgeons, a tent maker, an otter hunter, the keeper of the King's cows, the kings of heralds, a furrier to catch rabbits and a man employed to catch birds with glue. One of the surgeons had a groom who went into Carlisle to buy herbs for the King's feet and on 15 October four carts from Carlisle were

Lanercost Bridge once carried the main Carlisle to Newcastle Road.

hired to take wax, almonds, rice, cloth, canvas and spices to Lanercost. A small herd of goats was also in attendance, as Edward believed their milk was beneficial.

He was evidently a superstitious man as he kept a saint's tooth, which he believed protected him against thunder and lightning, and he also had a silver gilt vase, made in the form of a ship, which was said to contain the relics of 1,100 virgins! Not to be outdone in extravagance his son, Prince Edward, staying at nearby Wetheral, amused himself and his boisterous companions by hunting with his dogs, hawks and a pet lion.

During his stay Edward underlined his formidable reputation by having two brothers of Robert the Bruce hanged, drawn and quartered, and a steady supply of severed enemy heads was brought to the priory. He knew he was dying and he gave instructions that his body should be boiled and the bones put in a casket that would forever be carried in front of the English army until the Scots had been defeated. His heart was to be encased in a silver casket for burial in the Holy Land.

In March 1307 he left for Carlisle, aiming to cross the Solway at the Peat Wath just west of Rockliffe. He never made it. Within sight of his ancient enemy he died and his body was taken to nearby Burgh by Sands church, where it lay in state for 11 days. It was eventually taken back to London in a spectacular funeral cortege train accompanied by hundreds of noblemen and bodyguards. On 20 July Edward II was proclaimed King of England in Carlisle. He would suffer a disastrous defeat at Bannockburn seven years later.

Robert the Bruce decided to punish Lanercost for hosting his enemy so bountifully and in 1311 he seized the priory and had all the clergy put in prison. Still to be seen on the abbey walls are the black burn marks where his son David II lit huge fires around the walls.

To stave off poverty the abbot had to sell land and King Henry VIII took possession of it during the period of the Dissolution of the Monasteries, eventually handing it over to a layman – a Dacre of nearby Naworth Castle.

The ruins at the east end are a fine and impressive example of early Gothic architecture and the nave is still in use today as a parish church.

LONGTOWN

This is another Border town whose tranquil appearance belies its violent past. It was built on the site of a Roman camp on the nearby Netherby Hall and the area surrounding Longtown mostly belonged to the Graham family. Even among the lawless Border reiver families such as the Armstrongs, Bells, Johnstons and Elliotts they were notorious. By 1552 they had erected 15 pele towers in the Longtown area alone and the situation was so bad that both England and Scotland declared

Esk Bridge was built by the Grahams of Netherby in the mid 18th century.

In 1746 Bonnie Prince Charlie and his army crossed the Esk near Longtown, hotly pursued by an English army.

that they would 'lay waste' to the area, allowing the local citizens to rob, burn and murder. This no-go area eventually became known as 'the Debatable Land', effectively belonging to nobody. It wasn't until the accession of James VI of Scotland to the crown of England that peace was finally restored.

In 1745 another army came marching in from the north. This time it was the young Pretender Prince Charles Edward Stuart, Bonnie Prince Charlie of the ballads, who was risking all in his bid for the English crown. In 1746 he was on his way back, pursued by his cousin and arch enemy the Duke of Cumberland.

It was now winter and the clans crossed the river, even though it was running quite full, by linking arms and forming a barrier against the current. It was said that they were so delighted to be back in their own country that they lit fires to dry themselves on the Scottish bank and danced to the hundred or so bagpipers that had accompanied them on their journey.

By the mid-18th century the Grahams of

Netherby had built the Esk bridge, laid out the wide tree-lined streets of the town and built a coaching inn, the Graham Arms, at the main crossroads. It is not as bustling a place as it once was and the nearby M6 carries the traffic away from the town, but Longtown retains its elegance and its sense of history

MARYPORT

In the early 1700s Maryport was just a little fishing creek at the mouth of the River Ellen consisting of a few huts and a farmhouse. By the end of the century, thanks to a local businessman, Humphrey Senhouse, who needed a good harbour for the export of coal from his estate, it was a thriving port of 20,000 people. In 1749 an Act of Parliament was passed to allow the creation of the present town, which was renamed after his wife Mary.

Over the years various docks were added and the Senhouse dock, the largest, was opened in 1884. At the near end of the South Pier is another rarity, the old iron lighthouse – erected in 1846.

The origins of the town go back much further, however. Maryport began its life almost 2,000 years ago when the Romans arrived. On the 200ft high cliffs to the north-east of the town are the remains of a large Roman fort with gateways and defensive ditches still visible. It was probably called Alauna, and was built as a command and supply base for the coastal defences of Hadrian's Wall at its western extremity. It was the last in a series of forts guarding the northern frontiers against attack from the Picts to the north and the Irish from across the sea. Recently, geo-magnetic surveys have established that there was a large Roman town surrounding the fort. The first recorded occupant was a Roman officer called Marcus Maenius Agrippa, who was a personal friend of the Emperor Hadrian and at one time he commanded a cohort of Spaniards there. It was built around AD122, but there was an earlier fort, probably founded in Agricola's time in AD79, which was then built over. It was occupied for nearly 300 years until the army was recalled to defend Rome from the barbarians in AD410.

Maryport disappears from the record books after that, but it was probably colonised by the Vikings, whose tombs have been found a few miles to the north in Crosscanonby Church. As it was part of Scotland at the time it does not appear in the Domesday Book, and the next earliest clue can be found at Motte Hill – a 12th-century motte and bailey castle from the Norman period.

It was in the Victorian era that the town began to flourish, with coal mines and an iron foundry boosting its growth. The shipyards developed next to the docks and Maryport became famous for its ability to launch ships 'sideways' because of the narrowness of the River Ellen. The railway to Carlisle was built in the 1840s with George Stephenson as its engineer. Maryport was in its heyday and it was soon exporting huge quantities of coal. The town went into decline at the beginning of the 20th century, and during the depression in the 1930s adult unemployment reached 50 percent.

There was a brief recovery during World War Two, but afterwards many of the mines closed down, the final open-cast one closing in 2000. Today the town is looking a lot more confident, with a series of major regeneration projects under way.

Among its many famous sons Maryport includes Fletcher Christian, the *Bounty* mutineer. He was a master's mate on board *The*

*Bottom Left:
Roman Altars,
Senhouse Museum,
Maryport.*

*Below: Roman
Fort, Maryport.*

Port Carlisle was once a busy port with ships sailing to Liverpool and beyond from this now ruined quay.

Remains of the Dandy Railway Station platform can still be seen in Port Carlisle.

evident in the high 12in east window, which was used to fire arrows from. It claims to be the smallest church window in England and the 2ft 7in main door could be another record. The church, dedicated to St John the Baptist, was derelict for two centuries after the Dissolution of the Monasteries during the Reformation, but it was restored in the 19th century. There is a tradition that the church was built on the site of an earlier one founded by St Ninian, as a thank you for his safe return from Rome where he had been studying to be a priest.

PORT CARLISLE

Once a tiny hamlet called Fisher's Cross, Port Carlisle was the brainchild of Carlisle businessmen who were looking for a cheap and easy way to export their goods by sea. A canal was built from Carlisle and there were plans to build a link to Newcastle, but they never materialised. It was opened in March 1823 and boats towed passengers along the canal, reaching Port Carlisle in one hour 40 minutes. Larger ships were waiting to transport them to places such as Liverpool and even further afield. An elegant row of

Georgian houses was built; one of them, Solway House, was the hotel where they waited for the tides to turn.

Its most famous passenger was probably US President Woodrow Wilson's mother. Born in Carlisle, she emigrated from here across the Atlantic. Inevitably the canal became uneconomic and was drained in 1853 to be replaced by a steam railway line in 1854. This did not last long and was in turn replaced by the famous horse-drawn carriages known as Dandys, which travelled between Port Carlisle and Drumburgh. At the west end of the village, Hesket House has a small Roman altar stone set above the lintel bearing the words 'Matribus suis milite'. It was probably dedicated by a group of soldiers to the Mother Goddess. The dock and harbour, now splendidly decaying ruins, are excellent places to tread flounders or flat fish and the recently-opened Roman Wall path is reviving the bed and breakfast trade.

ROCKLIFFE

At the head of the River Eden stands Rockliffe village and its huge marsh, a famous stopover place for thousands of migrant geese and invading armies.

It gets its name from two old Norse words 'Rod' and 'Cliva', meaning red cliff, and until 1552 when the border was moved to the River Sark, the northern limit of its parish was the border between England and Scotland. It also used to be the main port for Carlisle.

There was once a castle here which commanded all the nearby fords and among the rules it was established that the warden should have at least 100 or 200 men 'nightlie

St Mary's Church, Rockcliffe stands on the site of an earlier 12th century building.

with him especially at the ebbinges of the water, some to watch at the fordes for the keepinge out of the Scottish thieves'.

It didn't keep out invading armies and Rockliffe was the Piccadily Circus of warring kings. Apart from the Romans and assorted Dark Age kings, the nearby fords were crossed by Edward I, Robert the Bruce and Charles Edward Stuart on his fateful way to Derby in 1745 with his Highland army.

Just outside the village there is a fine Grecian-style mansion house belonging to the Mounsey-Heysham family, who also inspired the building of the Church of St Mary – built in 1871 and erected on the site of a 12th-century one. A plaque inside is dedicated to the memory of Captain William Mounsey (1765–1830) of the Royal Navy, who, in 35 years of service, captured 31 enemy ships including the frigate *La Furieuse*, for which last action he received the thanks of the Admiralty and a special gold medal from George III. In the churchyard is a solid wheel

*An old Drovers'
road follows the
cliff tops at
Rockcliffe.*

head cross dating from the 10th or 11th century.

The tall church spire can be seen for miles around. On 8 November it was struck by lightning during a violent thunderstorm and had to be rebuilt.

Leading down to the church from the cliffs is an old drove road, once the main land route to Scotland, and it passes a pleasant pub, diplomatically called the Crown and Thistle.

Smuggling at Rockliffe

Smuggling was rife in the Borders during the middle of the last century. The different scales of duty levied on spirits in England and Scotland were the main reason for this. As whisky and brandy could be bought in Scotland and sold in England at five times the price, the temptation to indulge in smuggling was strong. At Rockliffe in the middle of the

last century, it was found necessary to keep a force of three or four excisemen. Their job was to watch all the roads that led from Springfield on the Scottish side of the Border and they also had the difficult task of keeping their eyes on Rockliffe marsh.

Most Rockliffe houses contained a tin canister shaped like a pair of women's corsets. Each was buckled with a leather strap and held a fair supply of 'mountain dew'. The result of this was a cheap supply of good whisky, which was available in Rockliffe houses when even bread was scarce.

The Rockliffe Ferry

Although there have been ferrymen and women at Rockliffe for almost 400 years, the earliest recorded name is of a Mr Carte, who, along with his wife, who was known as 'Bet o' the boat', was working the ferry during the 1800s.

The Drovers' road leading up to the village from Rockcliffe Marsh was once the main road into England.

An interesting footnote to the story concerns William Joyce, otherwise known as Lord Haw Haw, who sent broadcasts from Nazi Germany during World War Two. He had married a fellow blackshirt called Margo White from the Wigton road area of Carlisle and was a regular user of the ferry until it stopped in 1939.

During one of his 'Gairmany calling' rants he singled out the little village of Rockliffe with its ferry for special attention from bombers. He was later captured, tried for treason and hanged in London in 1946.

Over the centuries the vast 2,000 acres of Rockliffe marsh have been spreading outwards and the fine surface called Cumberland turf once graced the tennis courts of Wimbledon and Wembley stadium. It now doubles up as grazing ground for sheep and cattle and also as a nature reserve, where thousands of wild geese from the Arctic live during winter and spring. It is in private hands, however, and permission to wander on it has to be obtained beforehand. Needless to say it is also highly dangerous when the tides are running. Little mud-banked creeks can fill up in a matter of minutes to form deep and alarmingly wide channels of sea water…

The Boat House and Will o' The Boats

At the entrance to the marsh, just two miles north of Rockliffe, is a one-storey white-washed cottage. It was an inn for travellers risking the Solway crossings and a favourite haunt of smugglers. The innkeeper was Willie Irving, who also earned money as a guide or ferryman. Apparently many of his clients were runaway couples heading for Gretna Green. There is an old inn sign still hanging, which reads:

'Ere Metal Brig or Rail were thowt on,
Here Honest Will the Boatman rowt on.
Gentle and simple he did guide,
To either Scotch or English side.
Wi' them on horseback he did ride
An' boat the footman.
An' none did ever dread the tide
Wi' Will the Boatman.

Now tho' Will's work is done an' o'er
An' Will himself lies quiet,
Yet lives his Spirit here – step in an' try it,
Ne'er Time not Tide can half so pure supply it.'

SILLOTH

Silloth gets its name from the Norse hlada (barn). The monks from Holme Cultram Abbey stored their grain in barns known as 'lathes'. Because the lathes were by the sea they were known as sea lathes and over the centuries this was changed to Silloth. It came into prominence in the 1850s as the port and rail head for Carlisle and the British Railway Company imported imposing grey granite from Ireland in their own steamboats to build the main church.

The church enjoys spectacular views across the Solway and was fine enough to be painted by Joseph Turner. The town really came into its own in the 19th century when two docks were opened in 1859 and 1879. It is no longer used as a passenger port, but in 2007 it still has a small fishing fleet and the dock is in regular use.

It was a very popular Victorian holiday resort, noted for its clean, invigorating air. It was thought to be especially beneficial for chest complaints and was short-listed as suitable for the convalescence of King George V. The wide, elegant, cobbled streets and beautiful front and promenade were enjoyed by Carlisle holidaymakers until the 1950s. During the summer months between 1924 and 1936 groups of Carlisle children, many of whom had never seen the sea, were brought

The wide, elegant cobbled streets are a remarkable feature of Silloth.

to spend a day on the beach by local charities. Sadly, the main railway line connecting it to Carlisle was closed in 1963 by Doctor Beeching.

During World War Two Silloth was thought to be a 'safe' harbour and the docks were kept very busy. A large airfield brought in servicemen and women from all over the world. The hangars are still there and have now been taken over by enterprising businesses.

It is also well known for its championship links golf course and has been the venue for the English Ladies Amateur Open in its time. It was the home course of Miss Cecil Leitch (1871–1978), considered to be the most famous women golfer of all time. The incomparable post-war contralto Kathleen Ferrier, who first discovered her talent in Cumbria, used to play here occasionally as well. A plaque on the wall of the local bank marks the place where she lived during her marriage.

She did not seem to take golf too seriously and would occasionally throw her club after her ball to see if it would go further. Other famous players were the late Duke of Kent and Sir William Whitelaw. He was a cabinet minister under Margaret Thatcher. She placed great trust in him and once famously remarked that 'everyone should have a Willie…'

SKINBURNESS

It is hard to believe that this little collection of cottages was once one of the busiest ports in the west of England and a staging post for King Edward I's navy, affording places for over 400 ships. It was crucially important during his invasions of Scotland in 1299. It was from here that the Cistercian monks

The sea front in Silloth has wide, sweeping views of the Solway Firth.

from Holme Cultram Abbey developed a small fort to export wool from their large flocks of sheep. In the 13th century it was in its heyday as a thriving market town and a strategic naval station. It was a chartered burgh, had its own fairs and markets and a considerable trade with the rest of England and Ireland. Unfortunately, much of the village was washed away in a storm in 1301, which broke the sea dyke. The people moved to nearby Newton Arlosh. It still had its uses, though, and in the 19th century troops embarked here for the Crimean War.

In his novel *Redgauntlet*, Sir Walter Scott sets the scene of a surreptitious landing by Bonnie Prince Charlie, years after Culloden, where he meets a gathering of Jacobites at an inn with a quay. The inn became a smuggler's clearing house and local people used to speak of an underground tunnel connecting it with Abbeytown and Newton Arlosh. The name

Skinburness means 'the headland of the demon haunted castle', and the late professor Norma Goodrich, an American Arthurian scholar, claimed that Grune point, a two-mile long shingle spit, is the spot where Sir Gawain of Round Table fame had his fateful meeting with the Green Knight. It is now designated as an Area of Special Scientific Interest for bird life and marsh plants and is a favourite place for A-level geographers to study on field trips. Still surviving along the edge of the marsh is a mediaeval sea defence known as the Sea Bank.

WIGTON

The ancient settlement of Wigton sits halfway between the Solway and the Caldbeck fells to the south and was originally a Roman cavalry station called Maglona, or 'Old Carlisle'. The

Opposite: Christ's Church, Silloth in its wide, cobbled square.

affectionate local nickname for it is 'the throstle's nest' or 'thrush's nest'. The story goes that a soldier, returning from World War One, came over the brow of a hill and, overjoyed at seeing his home again, declared 'Away lads, it's the throstle's nest of all England.'

Ever since it received its Royal Market Charter in 1262 Wigton has been the focus of business and social life in what is known as the Cumbrian Plain, and markets are still held there today. Although the layout is mediaeval, most of the houses were built in the latter half of the 1700s when cotton and linen manufacturing, dyeing, printing and tanning industries brought prosperity, and much of the town is now a conservation area with many listed Georgian buildings clustered around the centre.

In the middle of the market place is the superb George Moore Memorial Fountain, built in 1872 by the man himself in memory of his wife Eliza. He was a poor ambitious apprentice of 19 who had travelled to London

from Wigton to seek his fortune and he fell in love with his master's daughter. She was a loving wife and charitable soul and the four bronze reliefs, the work of the Pre-Raphaelite sculptor Thomas Woolner, depict her favourite Acts of Mercy: *Visiting the Afflicted*, *Clothing the Naked*, *Instructing the Ignorant* and *Feeding the Hungry*.

Famous names associated with Wigton include broadcaster and author Melvyn Bragg and, earlier, Charles Dickens, who stayed at the King's Arms hotel with Wilkie Collins in 1857. They were on a tour described in *The Lazy Tour of Two Idle Apprentices*. Dickens was 'Francis Goodchild' and Collins, who had a sprained ankle, was 'Thomas Idle'. Continual rain had soured the men's views of Cumberland and Wigton but the following extract shows how little effect the weather had on the locals…

'Greatly ashamed of his splendid appearance, the conscious Goodchild quenched it as much as possible, in the

IN MEMORIAM.

Wigton in Cumbria – birthplace of author Melvyn Bragg.

shadow of Thomas Idle's ankle, and in a corner of the little covered carriage that started with them for Wigton – a most desirable carriage for any country, except for its having a flat roof and no sides; which caused the plumps of rain accumulating on the roof to play vigorous games of bagatelle into the interior all the way, and to score immensely. It was comfortable to see how the people coming back in open carts from Wigton market made no more of the rain than if it were sunshine; how the Wigton policeman taking a country walk of half-a-dozen miles (apparently for pleasure), in resplendent uniform, accepted saturation as his normal state; how clerks and schoolmasters in black, loitered along the road without umbrellas, getting varnished at every step; how the Cumberland girls, coming out to look after the Cumberland cows, shook the rain from their eyelashes and laughed it away; and how the rain continued to fall upon all, as it only does fall in hill countries.

'Wigton market was over, and its bare

booths were smoking with rain all down the street. Mr Thomas Idle, melodramatically carried to the inn's first floor, and laid upon three chairs (he should have had the sofa, if there had been one), Mr Goodchild went to the window to take an observation of Wigton, and report what he saw to his disabled companion.

"Brother Francis, brother Francis," cried Thomas Idle, "What do you see from the turret?"

"I see," said Brother Francis, "what I hope and believe to be one of the most dismal places ever seen by eyes. I see the houses with their roofs of dull black, their stained fronts, and their dark-rimmed windows, looking as if they were all in mourning. As every little puff of wind comes down the street, I see a perfect train of rain let off along the wooden stalls in the market-place and exploded against me. I see a very big gas lamp in the centre which I know, by a secret instinct, will not be lighted to-night. I see a pump, with a trivet underneath its spout whereon to stand the vessels that are brought to be filled with water. I see a man come to pump, and he pumps very hard, but no water follows, and he strolls empty away.'"

The town can't have been as dull as Dickens described, as there are records of Market Hill being the scene of cockfighting, bear-baiting, religious meetings and Chartist riots in its time, and during the celebrations to mark the victory at Trafalgar in 1805 the wooden cross in the Market Square was accidentally burned down. The locals certainly knew how to party...

Other Wigton notables were the Revd John Ford, father of Anna Ford the broadcaster, who did much to restore St Mary's Church, and John Woodcock Graves, who wrote the song *John Peel*.

If you do go to visit be prepared for some interesting words that pepper the local dialect. The gypsies or 'Potters' who lived in the East End of the town spoke Romany, which etymologists believe had its origin in Indian languages, and these words were in common use in Carlisle even within living memory. 'Kushti' or 'Baary' meant good, 'Mort' or 'Mot' meant woman, 'Radj' meant bad and 'Gadgie' meant man.

For about 300 years, well after the pacification of the Borders in 1603, Wigton was also the site of the famous Rosley Fair. From all over Scotland and Cumbria farmers would congregate for a tryst or selling fair at Whitsuntide and other times in high summer. The drovers, with thousands of cattle, horses and sheep, would have travelled from as far away as the Highlands of Scotland to sell their beasts, crossing the Solway from a point near Annan or Dornock and meeting up at Rosley, about four miles south-east of Wigton. Having bought their animals the farmers would feed them over winter and fatten them up before heading south to the great southern markets such as Smithfield in London.

These must have been fantastic occasions, as it wasn't just the farmers who were looking for a deal. Hawkers, gypsies, tailors, saddlers, jewellers and fruit sellers were all out and about. If you were thirsty there were gallons of ale and nut sellers, fruit merchants and gingerbread cakes were all doing business. Other lively and colourful markets would have been at Brough Hill in Westmoreland and Stagshawbank near Hexham.

Overleaf:
Dryfe Sands, near Lockerbie.

The Scottish Side of the Solway

*Annan Waterfoot —
the sea wall.*

*Annan Waterfoot —
Robbie Burns
plaque.*

ANNAN WATERFOOT

In a letter to a friend, Mrs Francis Dunlop, in 1792, Burns described Annan Waterfoot as 'this wild place of the world'. It was a small landing jetty on the River Nith estuary rather than a harbour and ships simply beached and were refloated at high tides. Burns would have spent a considerable amount of time here in his capacity as an exciseman, checking the cargoes of the vessels being unloaded onto carts and packhorses. In the 18th and 19th century thousands of people embarked from the jetty bound for Canada, New Zealand and Australia.

Waterfoot Farm on the Newbie side of the river gave accommodation to travellers waiting for the ferry to Cumbria and cattle drovers would wait for low tide before crossing over. Every year huge numbers of cattle, sometimes as many as 60,000 in a few months, would be driven across on their way to the markets in the south of England.

Travelling from Ayrshire and Galloway they would avoid the toll bridges at Dumfries and Carlisle by keeping to the east of the river Nith.

The inn at Waterfoot Farm had deep cellars useful for storing smuggled goods, but it was unfortunately destroyed in the 1970s.

THE ROYAL BURGH OF ANNAN

In 1127 King David of Scotland awarded all of Annandale to a powerful Norman family called the de Brus, or the Bruces, who already held lands in Yorkshire. The first royal charter was granted by Robert Bruce in 1306 and was confirmed by later monarchs, but the charter document was destroyed during the Border wars when the town was sacked several times by the English. King James V reinstated the town in 1538 and each year on the first Saturday in July there are celebrations involving a riding of the marches or boundaries, massed pipe bands and sports events. On the edge of the main channel of the Solway is a large boulder called the Altar Stone, and it is visited by the riders as it marks the seaward boundary of the Royal Burgh.

There is some doubt about where Annan gets its name from. There was a Roman settlement called Veronum here in AD120 but the word Anu could be linked to the Celtic goddess of prosperity, or the Gaelic word for a slow flowing river.

Some of Annan's famous sons include Hugh Clapperton (1788–1827), the explorer of West Africa, and Edward Irving

The Port, Annan.

(1792–1834), the founder of the Catholic Apostolic Church (the Irvingites). From 1814 to 1816 Thomas Carlyle taught mathematics at Annan Academy, where he met and befriended Irving, who was also a teacher there. While Daniel Defoe described the town on a visit as being in a 'state of irrevocable decay', Carlyle thought Annan 'a fine bright self-confident little town'.

Annan was at one time a flourishing port and in the 19th century ships sailed from here

Annan Town Hall.

Dryfe Sands, the scene of one of the bloodiest battles in Scottish History.

to Liverpool, the Baltic and America. It was also a major point for emigration and there are the remains of two piers where families caught boats for the new world across the Atlantic.

Originally a small market town, Annan developed into a considerable ship-building centre and in 1898 Cochran and Company of Birkenhead brought jobs and prosperity, reflected in the impressive red sandstone buildings of the main streets. They eventually specialised in producing gigantic boilers so large they had to be floated down the Solway to their destinations. Sadly the industry declined, as did the fishing. In 1896 Annan could boast a fleet of 51 shrimp trawlers, 30 whammel boats, 13 herring boats and 24 smaller boats. Within three years they had almost entirely disappeared. Traditional methods of fishing such as Gowesk netting, haaf netting, stake traps and poke nets are still in use, but they are fighting a battle for survival.

BATTLE OF DRYFE
SANDS 1593

This was the last full-scale battle fought on the Borders and was essentially a family fight between the Johnstones and Maxwells. These two great Dumfriesshire surnames, the one inhabiting Nithsdale and the other Annandale, were bitter enemies. George Macdonald Fraser in *The Steel Bonnets* claims that theirs was the bitterest and bloodiest family quarrel in British history, including even those of the Highlands.

The families feature regularly in accounts

of raids into England and they were permanent rivals for the position of Warden of the West March. Successive Scottish kings were aware of this and played a game of 'your turn next', to the annoyance of both. The heads of both families were regularly in and out of prison and needless to say, when a Maxwell was appointed as a warden he would get little cooperation from a Johnstone and vice versa.

The overture to the actual battle is highly complex, with raid leading to counter-raid and the wardenship at one point being awarded to whoever might be able to survive the longest. A flavour of the times comes from accounts of what might be a typical foray. When John Johnstone was appointed warden, Robert Maxwell, with 400 Armstrongs, Scotts, Beatties and Littles, sacked the Johnstone castle of Lockwood, killed six men, took 12 prisoners and then burned the castle 'that lady Johnstone might have a light to put on her hood'.

The Johnstones gave as good as they got and struck back with raids on Annan and Dumfries, burning a dozen Maxwell villages, stealing 400 cattle and sacking the estate of Applegarth. When John Johnstone died King James appointed Robert Maxwell as the new warden, despite the fact that James had only a few years before Maxwell imprisoned him and had 22 of his kinsmen executed.

A particularly brutal raid by the Johnstones into Nithsdale resulted in a group of widows travelling to Edinburgh to petition the king. They took with them 15 bloody shirts belonging to their dead husbands. They were refused an audience but their demonstration in the streets made such an impression on public opinion that James was forced to act.

He ordered the warden, Maxwell, to arrest Johnstone of Dunskellie and, if he would not surrender, attack his castle of Lochwood and 'raze out the memory of him and his name in these bounds'. Official sanction was just what Maxwell needed and he set off with a 2,000-strong force to carry out his instructions to the letter.

He also announced a £10 reward in land to anyone who could bring him Johnstone's head or hand. Johnstone, not quite as wealthy, offered £5 in response for a portion of Maxwell. Johnstone assembled a mixed band of 400 of his own clan and additions of Elliots, Scotts, Irvines and English Grahams. The presence of an 11-year-old rider, one Robert Johnstone of Raecleuch, in their ranks showed just how desperate their position was, but when Maxwell reached the River Annan at a point just below its junction with Dryfe water he found his enemy ready and waiting.

He lured the vanguard into an ambush with a frontal attack and drove it back into Maxwell's main force, and the battle surged back and forth into the streets of the town itself. The Johnstones were fighting for their lives on home territory and they began to cut Maxwell's force to pieces. Anyone not on a horse was at dangerous disadvantage and many suffered a downward blow to the face, rather than the usual leg wounds. These injuries were later to be known as a 'Lockerbie lick'. Maxwell himself was thrown from his horse and, being a tall man and weighed down with heavy armour, he could not rise to his feet. It is not quite clear who killed him, but one version of the story goes that he held out his hand to surrender and his arm was cut off. This was then carried away and nailed to the wall of Lochwood castle.

The Maxwells lost 700 men in the encounter but the Johnstones were outlawed and they too had suffered heavy losses. Two years later, astonishingly, James Johnstone was appointed warden and he was the last one to serve in that office. The feud lingered on for another 15 years, though, and the denouement was predictable.

In 1608 a truce was proposed and elaborate efforts to avoid violence were put in place. The then Lord Maxwell and James Johnstone met with single attendants and Maxwell shot Johnstone twice in the back. He was forced to flee to France where he stayed for four years, but when he returned to Scotland he was betrayed and executed.

It ended an appalling, long-running vendetta in which four clan chiefs and hundreds of their followers had been killed.

BROW WELL

Robbie Burns came here in 1796 to cure what his friend Dr Maxwell had diagnosed as 'flying gout'. The well, nine miles to the south-east of Dumfries, was noted for its 'medicinal' waters which contain iron salts, but it is doubtful if they were any help to the dying man. Burns was at a low ebb. The war with France was causing food shortages in Britain, the harvest of 1795 had failed and in March 1796 there were serious food riots in Dumfries. Because of his poor health Burns had had his salary reduced and he became obsessed with the fear of poverty.

He had recently received a solicitor's letter for non-payment of a tailor's account for his volunteer's uniform and a terror of dying in a debtor's prison gripped him. He wrote a

The Brow Well — Robert Burns visited here for his health.

desperate letter to his friend George Thomson for money. 'A cruel scoundrel of a Haberdasher, to whom I owe an account, taking it into his head that I am dying has commenced a process and will infallibly put me in jail. Do for God's sake send me five pounds.'

Burns stayed at Brow Well from 3 July until 18 July. He was advised to bathe in sea water and each day he waded out shoulder deep into the cold Solway. A current theory is that he was suffering from rheumatic heart disease and if he had been then this would only have made matters worse. His doctor had also recommended port wine as a tonic, but the penniless Burns could not afford it. The generous landlady of the Clarencefield Inn where he was staying provided him with an ample supply and refused payment. Another friend, Mrs Maria Riddle, who was also in the district recovering from illness, invited Burns to dinner at her lodgings and she remembered that Burns asked her if she had any message he could take to the other world for her…he obviously knew that he was dying. He returned to Dumfries and on

The Brow Well, a well-used spa near Dumfries.

the morning of Thursday 21 July he became delirious. His children were brought to see him for the last time and shortly afterwards he lapsed into unconsciousness and died. He was only 37 years old.

BURNSWARK

Burnswark Hill is capped by an Iron Age Fort.

From the English side of the Solway the flat-topped mound of Burnswark looks like a large capsized boat, but it is a natural feature of the landscape with quite a history. There

are the remains of a British Iron Age fort covering some 17 acres at the summit, indicating that it was possibly a centre of resistance against the Romans. Whether it was involved in a siege is unclear, but there are large Roman marching camps on both the north and south sides and three ballista platforms dominate the northern ramparts. These were probably used as target practice areas, as several examples of leaden sling-shot have been recovered from the area during excavation. This theory is supported by the fact that there are also practice earthworks nearby where Roman engineers would have taught the troops the rudiments of trench digging.

On a less prosaic level, the place has mystical qualities and the eastern outcrop is called the Fairy Crag by locals. They tell the story of the young girl from a nearby village called Corrie, who was abducted by the fairies. Her parents thought she was lying dead in her bed but this was just a fairy trick, as her brother discovered when he had a vision of where she really was. She told him that to rescue her he would have to go to their barn that night and wait until midnight when three figures would walk past…he was to grab the third one (which would be her) and repeat some words she would give him. Unfortunately, he was too scared to go and she was stuck with the fairies…forever…

It is possible that a great battle was fought here in 937. A Saxon King, Athelstan, defeated a huge mixed army of Picts and Scots at a place called 'Brunanburh' in 'the north'. Nobody seems to know where this might be, but Burnswark is a very likely spot. The battle is commemorated in a long poem in *The Anglo-Saxon Chronicle* and describes Viking survivors fleeing westwards to Dublin in their longboats.

CAERLAVEROCK CASTLE

This imposing ruin stands sentinel at the mouth of the River Nith, seven miles south of Dumfries. It would have dominated the

whole region and as such was a prime target for invading armies. Its story begins with the granting of land to Sir John De Maccuswell in 1220. It was just about complete in 1300 and saw almost immediate action when Edward I invaded southern Scotland and laid siege to it with over 800 men. He had a huge collection of siege engines brought in from all over southern Scotland and northern England, and the castle was eventually taken. It must have been quite an

The unusual Caerlaverock Castle was once a stronghold of the powerful Maxwell family.

Caelaverock Castle – a romantic ruin in a picturesque setting.

Barnacle Geese spend the winter on the salt marshes at Caerlaverock.

operation, as the triangular shape, boggy marsh and surrounding moat would have presented the besiegers with severe problems.

The castle remained in English hands until 1312, but Scottish suspicions about the Maxwells' loyalty to the Crown led to it being besieged again in 1356. It was constantly changing hands, with more attacks from the English in 1544 and 1570, and it was not until the Union of the Crowns in 1603 that there was any significant peace.

In 1634 Robert Maxwell, the First Earl of Nithsdale, began to domesticate the castle, making it more of a residence than a fighting unit. He built the magnificent Nithsdale Lodging which now dominates the interior.

But there was more trouble to come. The English Civil War spilled over into Scotland and the country was ravaged by wars of religion, doctrine and kingship. The Maxwells took the Royalist side, supporting King Charles I against a besieging army of Covenanters for 13 weeks before eventually surrendering. There was significant damage done during the siege and the castle was never repaired properly. It was placed in state care in 1946 and is now looked after by Historic Scotland.

CAERLAVEROCK WILDFOWL AND WETLANDS TRUST CENTRE

The trust was founded by the late Sir Peter Scott and the 1,400-acre wild nature reserve centre was opened in the autumn of 1970. There is a long history of wild fowling in the Solway area and the numbers of wild geese, particularly the barnacles, had declined to a point where they were in danger of being wiped out.

From a population of fewer than 500 there are now vast flocks of more than 25,000. In autumn they arrive from the high Arctic archipelago of Svalbard and they roost on the saltflats and merses until about April when they fly back. Whooper swans swoop in from Iceland and huge numbers of ducks and wading birds from as far away as West Africa and Russia congregate here as well. Circling the flocks are the predators: peregrines, hen harriers and sparrowhawks.

CARSETHORN

Now a quiet little village with breathtaking views of the Solway, Carsethorn was once the last link with Scotland for thousands of emigrants. In 1850 10,000 people set sail from here to North America, 7,000 to Australia, and 4,000 to New Zealand. Among those 'travelling' to Australia were convicts who were marched down to Carsethorn from nearby Dumfries. They were kept waiting in a whitewashed building called the Barracks, which can still be seen today.

It was the Vikings who first established Carsethorn as a fishing and trading port where the hard shoreline gave them a safe place at low tide to beach their flat-bottomed ships.

In 1562 it was mentioned as a link between Scotland and Bordeaux and it established itself as the main port for Dumfries, particularly when the deep water channel of the River Nith moved closer to the village.

It was busiest in the late 1840s, with almost 25,000 tons of shipping entering the river. Trading links were especially strong with Liverpool, Ireland, the Isle of Man and Archangel in the north. Inevitably, the arrival of the railways and the high costs of keeping a deep enough channel open for the larger ships meant that by the early 1900s a final decline in sea trade set in.

It was highly probable that there was a good deal of smuggling going on during its heyday as a port. There are records of one member of the Blackett family of Arbigland who played the double game as an exciseman or 'Gauger'. He informed on some of the fellow smugglers who then informed on him, and he was forced to resign.

The founder of the American navy, John Paul Jones, who was born nearby, sailed from Carsethorn to England at the age of 13. He learned his trade in the merchant navy before impressing the American authorities during the revolutionary war with flamboyant attacks on British ships and territories, including one raid on the home of the Earl of Selkirk at Kirkudbright. He founded the US navy and later served with the Russian navy under Catherine the Great.

A worrying recent development has been the revival of the cockling trade. The local cocklemen have been slow to take up the granting of licences and commercial firms have filled the gap. The recent tragedy in Morecambe Bay where illegal Chinese workers were drowned has highlighted the problem of unlicensed criminal gangs raiding the beds. The coastguard and local police are only too aware that these gangs know nothing of the dangerous tides and quicksands.

Nearby is the unusual Kirkbean Church with a dome, a sundial giving the times in Calcutta, Gibralter and Madras, (places where local men were working in Victorian times) and a font presented by the US navy in memory of John Paul Jones.

Ships sailed to the New World from Carsethorn.

Right: The Clock Tower, Castle Douglas.

Far right: Jaqueline Shackleton's sculpture of Sir Peter Scott, founder of the Wildfowl Trust.

CASTLE DOUGLAS

Until 1792 this historic market town was known as Causewayend, on the shores of Carlingwark Loch, and it changed its name when Sir William Douglas laid out a new village on the site of the old one. The village had traded on the mining of marl, much used in the 18th century as a fertiliser. Sir William also established mills, but they could not compete with the newer ones opening up in Lanarkshire. He had started off as a pedlar in Lanarkshire and then grew rich in the early days of the Virginia trade. Robert Burns was

Mute Swans on the loch, Castle Douglas.

not impressed with what he saw as his self importance, and he lambasted Sir William in one of his poems.

There is a legend that the famous cannon 'Mons Meg', now on show in Edinburgh Castle, was used in the siege of nearby Threave Castle, blowing off the hand of the Fair Maid of Galloway in the process when she was sipping her wine.

From the 1600s Castle Douglas had benefitted from being on the route of the military road built by King James VI to Portpatrick to support the Ulster plantation, and the numerous hotels in the town underline its importance as a coaching stop during the 18th century.

It is still a thriving market town and it was once famous for the great October sales of pedigree Ayrshires. This tradition of providing quality fare is continuing and the town has set out its stall as a centre for high-quality produce with over 50 local businesses selling food and drink.

COMLONGON CASTLE

Comlongon Castle is a massive five-storey 15th-century tower with walls four metres thick in places. It is situated nine miles east of Dumfries and was built to combat the English, who would dash across the Solway fords to raid the area. The builders were the Murrays of Cockpool, who became the Earls of Annandale in the 1400s. Ever since it has stood witness to generations of violent Border disputes between the several powerful families that dominated the region.

It was a very safe place to live in as there was a very small entrance and the whole edifice was enclosed by a moat. Inside there was a rabbit warren of connecting chambers and underneath was a dungeon pit where prisoners were held for ransom – part of everyday Border business… The ransoms were usually paid in the form of sheep or cattle and many families were able to enrich their

Comlongon Castle was extended from a border tower built by the Murray family.

The gibbet on the wall at Comlongon Castle is a grim reminder of reiving times.

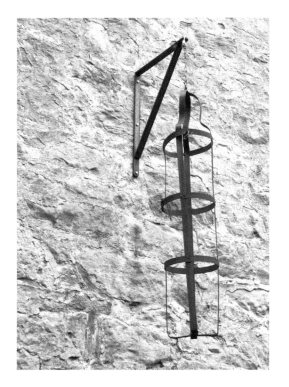

fortunes considerably. The entrance is through a doorway in the north wall, which still contains its original iron protective gate or yett, leading to the basement containing a fresh water well. From the basement a spiral staircase leads to the Great Hall, which is dominated by a vast fireplace with the Royal Arms of Scotland carved above it. Above the fireplace lintel are unusual carvings showing various plants and heads emanating from a dragon's breath, believed to depict the ancient Celtic legend of the Green Man or God of Spring.

In the early 18th century the descendants of the Murray family had a mansion house built adjacent to the castle. This was partly destroyed by fire in the late 19th century and was rebuilt in 1901.

The granite Town Hall in Dalbeattie.

The harbour, Dalbeattie.

The castle is said to be haunted by the ghost of a young woman who committed suicide there by jumping from the battlements. In 1536 Lady Marion Carruthers was forced into marriage with James Douglas of Drumlanrigg, a man she did not love. Marion had inherited half of the Mouswald estate nearby after the death of her father and Douglas had obtained consent to marry her and thus get part of it. Marion tried to escape by seeking sanctuary in Comlongon but a Privy Council ruling forced her hand and in desperation she killed herself. In other versions of the story she was murdered by the Douglas family for refusing the marriage.

Strange things are alleged to have happened in recent times with doors opening and closing, fireboards creaking and lights going on and off in empty rooms. An American couple staying at the castle opened their room to find a young girl sitting on their bed. They left thinking they had the wrong room but returned a short while later to find that the girl had vanished.

Of other ghoulish interest is that three mummified cats were discovered buried in the thick walls of the castle. Nobody seems to know why but they were possibly placed there as some sort of good luck sacrifice. This does not seem to put people off at all and the castle is currently a very popular hotel, owned and run by the Ptolemy family.

DALBEATIE

The town originally started as a coastal port and it wasn't until 1793 that it began to grow as a mill town and granite quarrying centre as well. The two main families in the area, the Maxwells of Munchies and the Copelands of Colliston, helped to develop the town on the grid system that is reflected in its present layout. The quarrying reached its peak in the 1870s and many of the imposing granite buildings in the town date from this period. It has still got its Craignair Hill quarry, but the Beeching railway cuts in the 1960s had a devastating affect on local businesses and now most of the town's income is from tourism and service industries.

BUITTLE CASTLE

The coastline around Dalbeattie is dotted with ancient forts and duns. In the post-Roman era

Buittle Castle.

a pilgrim route ran along the north shore of the Solway to the shrine of St Ninian at Whithorn. The Iron Age duns at Castle Point at Rockliffe and the Motte of Mark near Kippford could possibly have been strongholds of the post-Roman kingdom of Rheged.

Nearby is Buittle Tower, standing slightly above the site of the castle which used to belong to the ancient MacFergus family. They were so wealthy and powerful that King David I of Scotland recognised them as allies rather than subjects and they were to play a key role in the history of the country. They founded three abbeys in the area: Dundrennan in 1146, Glenluce in 1189 and Sweetheart Abbey in the 1200s. Lady Devorguilla founded Sweetheart as a burial place for her beloved husband and her son John Balliol II became an unwilling pawn in King Edward I's plans to conquer the country.

Edward appointed him King of Scotland and for a brief moment Buittle Castle became the most important place in the land. When Balliol showed signs of rebellion Edward had him stripped of his crown, sceptre and royal robes and the humiliated man was ever afterwards known as 'John twn tabard', or 'the man without a coat'. The castle was later sacked

and power passed to the Black Douglas clan, who entrenched themselves in Threave Castle near Castle Douglas.

DEVIL'S PORRIDGE

During World War One Britain was losing ground to Germany and was in desperate need of ammunition. The government arranged for a huge factory to be built between Dornock and Gretna. It would produce cordite on a massive scale and because of the danger of explosions the units were spread out over a distance of nine miles.

At its peak it employed 30,000 men and women with an output that was more than all the other munitions factories in Britain combined. It had 125 miles of its own railway network, 34 engines, an electric power station and a water treatment plant that could provide 10 million gallons a day.

The cordite had to be mixed by hand and involved a highly explosive combination of nitro-glycerine and nitro-cotton. The dried paste was processed into cordite and looked like uncooked spaghetti. It was then put into bullets and shells to propel them. When Sir Arthur Conan Doyle, creator of *Sherlock Holmes*, visited the factory in Gretna in 1918, he described the paste as 'the Devil's porridge.'

DRUMCOLTRAM TOWER

Drumcoltram Tower was built by Edward Maxwell, a younger son of Lord Maxwell, in the 1550s. It is a typical Border defensive structure built on the north slope of a valley

Drumcoltran Tower was built by the powerful Maxwells.

Drumcoltran Tower can be found along a quiet country road between Dumfries and Dalbeattie.

controlling the main road from Dumfries to Dalbeattie. It did not have any serious strategic importance and had various owners before passing by marriage to Captain John Maxwell of Cardoness in 1750. A Latin motto over the door reads 'Conceal secrets, be timid of speech, be truthful, beware of wine, remember death, be pitiful.'

It is now part of a working farm and is looked after by Historic Scotland. It is worth a visit as it has superb views from its 40ft parapet, set at the top of a wide spiral staircase.

DUNDRENNAN ABBEY

Dundrennan Abbey was once the home of an order of Cistercian Monks.

This ancient Cistercian Abbey was the scene of one of the most poignant moments in Scottish history when Edward Maxwell, the last abbot, welcomed Mary Queen of Scots to spend her last night on Scottish soil. The next day, 16 May 1586, she set sail in a small fishing boat for Workington across the Solway and then went on to Carlisle Castle. Once on English soil she was a dead woman and she was eventually executed at Fotheringay nine months later on the orders of her cousin Queen Elizabeth I.

The abbey was founded in 1142 by King David I, who invited monks from Rievaulx Abbey in Yorkshire to set up a daughter house in Galloway. The name (Dun-nan droigheann) translates from the Gaelic as 'fort or hill of the thorn bushes.' It would have taken about 50 years or more to complete, and the building work would have been undertaken by only about 23 monks and laymen, an astonishing feat.

The Cistercians lived a life of strict discipline, prayer and work. Their daily round would have started at 1.30am with regular services in the church and work on their farms. They would have looked after and employed many lay brothers and local men, exporting wool to the Continent from their own little port at nearby Burnfoot.

The abbey suffered a decline during the Reformation and abbots were replaced by commendators (administrators) appointed

by the current king or queen. In 1587 it passed to the Crown and in 1621 it was taken over by the Royal Chapel at Stirling. By this time the place was beginning to turn into a ruin and many of its stones were used to build houses in Dundrennan village. It wasn't until 1842 that steps were taken to preserve what was left of the building.

The cruciform church had a nave of six bays 130ft long, and a choir 45ft long. There was also a central tower 200ft high. The finest remains architecturally are those of the Chapter House, with a beautiful arched doorway between two windows and a roof supported by octagonal columns.

The village of Dundrennan was the location for the cult film *The Wicker Man* in 1972. It starred Christopher Lee, Britt Ekland and Edward Woodward, and it has since become a place of pilgrimage for thousands of 'Wickerfans'.

GLENCAPLE, NEAR DUMFRIES

Glencaple is an attractive small port on the shore of the River Nith about five miles southeast of Dumfries. It was founded in 1747 and served as a small seaside resort for the people of Dumfries because of its attractive setting with stunning views across the Nith towards Criffel. At one time there was a small shipbuilding industry here, but it had all but died out by the end of the 19th century. The village port's main function, however, was to

Mary, Queen of Scots was once a guest at Dundrennan Abbey.

Glencaple was once a busy port but its throughput is now greatly reduced.

allow ships that were unable to sail right up the Nith into Dumfries to unload their cargoes. Coal, lime and tobacco, as well as the more exotic cargoes of brandy, wine, dried fruits and rare textiles from Europe were all unloaded here – unfortunately, some of these valuable imports led to a thriving smuggling industry on the Solway and the customs officers suffered a continual and thankless struggle against these lawbreakers.

There were also shipments of grain, potatoes and livestock exported to various

The Village of Glencaple looks out onto The Solway Firth.

ports in England and Europe.

In the early 1800s there was an increase in the number of people emigrating to the colonies, particularly Canada, and there were regular sailings from Glencaple and also from Carsethorn.

In the late 1800s several combined factors led to a decrease in trade: the cost of improvements to the channel was prohibitive, a new dock opened at Silloth and because of increasing debts the Nith Navigation Commission extinguished the light at Southerness to save money, resulting in an accident in the river involving the tugboat *Arabian*, which saw the owner successfully sue the commission for financial compensation, plunging them into insolvency. The 20th century saw an almost complete decline – World War One brought river trade almost to a standstill and this was further exacerbated by World War Two.

There is still the occasional cargo brought into Glencaple but by and large it is now a sleepy little country harbour that enjoys a superb position on the beautiful banks of the historic River Nith.

Southerness Lighthouse was once extinguished as part of an economy drive!

The harbour at Glencaple.

Hoddom Castle is now the centre of a caravan park but was originally the home of the Maxwells.

HODDOM CASTLE AND REPENTANCE TOWER

In the shadow of Burnswark stands Hoddom Castle, which belonged for most of its existance to the Maxwell family. Earlier occupants included the Anglo Norman Hoddom family, who were granted lands here when Robert the Bruce was appointed to the Lordship of Annandale by King David I. For a while a branch of the Border Irvings was also involved.

The castle was built near an ancient religious site. In AD573 St Kentigern was recalled from Wales by King Rhydderch and he established his Episcopal See here before returning to Glasgow. Although there are only a few fragments of early Christian crosses here, it remained a place of religious significance for over a thousand years. The castle was mainly built by Sir John Maxwell in the 1560s, but there is evidence of earlier foundations, and it was considered to be one of the strongest and most important fortresses in the Borders. With walls nine feet thick it was virtually impregnable at the time.

The castle changed hands several times and in the 19th century it was owned by the Brook family, who employed an architect called William Burn to 'modernise' it. He turned it into a Victorian mansion. Sadly, the place was never lived in and it fell into disuse until World War Two, when Allied servicemen lived in it for a while. Since then the Victorian additions have been taken down and the castle is once more looking a bit like its old self.

Repentance Tower is eerily sited at the edge of an ancient graveyard on the site of an old chapel.

Opposite: Hoddom Church was destroyed by fire in February 1975 and is now an enigmatic ruin.

Hollows Tower once belonged to the notorious Black Jock , better known as Johnnie Armstrong of Gilnockie.

Half a mile away to the south is Repentance Tower. This was linked to the castle as a look-out post for the major part of the West March. Standing on the top of Trailtrow Hill it had a commanding prospect over much of lower Annandale and the Solway plain, including the two invasion routes into south-west Scotland. At the first sign of trouble a large beacon would be lit and within a few minutes places as far away as Edinburgh and Glasgow would be alerted as other beacons repeated the signal.

Nobody is quite sure why it is called 'repentance', but popular tradition has it that when the tower was built by Lord Herries he demolished a chapel there to provide building material. The powerful Archbishop of Glasgow was so incensed by what he saw as the desecration of a Christian site, a one-time seat of his predecessor St Kentigern, that he insisted on 'repentance'.

HOLLOWS TOWER OF GILNOCKIE

This is believed to be one of six pele towers belonging to Johnnie Armstrong of Gilnockie, a man viewed as semi-heroic in the Border Ballads but heartily detested on the English side, where he ran a successful protection racket and was a literal law unto himself.

It is now a Clan Armstrong centre, re-roofed and restored, and is a perfect example of how a pele tower might have looked. It was built in around 1520, about two miles north of Canonbie, and the oldest part of it, the large stone by the doorway into the basement, is thought to date from the second millennium BC, with carvings of spirals and a key-like symbol clearly visible.

It has four storeys plus an attic and massively thick walls, making it almost impregnable. The typical pele tower was built with a shrewd eye to defence. There would be only one entrance and that would be a double door at ground level, one being an outer door of iron grating and the inner one oak reinforced with more iron. There would be one spiral staircase, always built clockwise, going up, to favour a right-handed defender who would attack the exposed right side on an intruder. The exception to this was the Kerr family, who were usually left-handed and built theirs anti-clockwise. Interestingly, the slang word for left-handed is still 'car', 'cack' or 'ker' handed in the Borders today.

Animals would be herded into the bottom floor, living quarters were upstairs and at the very top would be a beacon ready to be lit at the first sign of a raid. The pele towers were not built to withstand a long siege, but as a defence against the usual hit and run forays they were superb. The defenders would bolt the doors, withdraw upstairs and shoot from narrow arrow slits in the walls. Anything handy on the roof could also be hurled down on the attackers. One ploy the attackers did have in their favour was the tactic of 'scumfishing', or piling straw against the doors and trying to smoke the defenders out. If there was a large-scale invasion force coming his way and his pele had to be abandoned, the Reiver had an ingenious plan to make sure it was not destroyed. He would stuff the interior full of smouldering peat, which meant that it was impossible for the attackers to lay gunpowder, or even get inside to blow it up. When things had quietened

Hollows Tower, once a stronghold of the notorious Armstrong family.

down the pele would still be standing and all that had to be done was to renew the woodwork.

Such was the tower belonging to Johnnie Armstrong, who would have one of the best-known ballads of the Border written about him…

Although Armstrong claimed that he only terrorised on the English side, he came to the attention of King James V, who was losing patience with what he saw as all-too powerful mercenaries on his southern border. He had already lambasted his nobles in Edinburgh during the winter of 1530 for failing to keep order and with a force of 10,000 men he swept south to deal with the Reivers once and for all, aiming straight for Liddlesdale, the Armstrong heartland.

According to the ballad Johnnie was invited by the king to attend a meeting at Carlenrig at the head of Teviotdale. There was no hint of a trap and he probably thought he was under some form of truce because he attended with 50 of his followers in the

equivalent of their Sunday best. James was astonished at the richness of their clothing and possibly irritated by the arrogant manner in which they conducted themselves. Whatever actually happened next is not clear, but it seems he took an instant dislike to Armstrong and ordered his men to arrest him on the spot.

Armstrong went straight into bargaining mode, pleading for his life and offering to bring James any English subject from a duke to a commoner dead or alive. This probably only made things worse and he was spirited away. He didn't go gently, and shouted his defiance:

'I am but a fool to seek grace at a graceless face. But had I known, Sir, that you would have taken my life this day, I should have lived on the Borders in spite of King Harry and you both, for I know King Harry would down-weigh my best horse with gold to know that I were condemned to die this day.'

Brave words, but south of the Border they breathed sighs of relief that there was one less cut-throat for them to worry about at night. There was no trial and the whole group was promptly hanged from the nearest trees. They were lucky: Sandie Scott, one of Armstrong's followers, was burned alive because he had, earlier in his career, burned a house containing a woman and her child.

The executions caused outrage throughout the Borders, mainly because it was thought that the king had abused the traditions of a truce, one of the few unwritten laws that a Reiver could be trusted to honour.

At Carlenrig, beside the church and enclosed by railings, are the graves of Johnnie Armstrong and his men. The inscription on a stone remembrance tablet says that he 'was treacherously murdered by a jealous King.' The official records in Edinburgh allow him two brief lines,

'John Armstrong, alias "Blak Jok" and Thomas his brother convicted of common theft, and reset of theft etc,-Hanged.'

Kirkbean Church.

JOHN PAUL JONES

(1747–1792)

Born in Arbigland, south of Dumfries, John Paul Jones is famous in the United States as the 'father of the American Navy', and a hero of the American Revolution. He also became an admiral in the Imperial Russian Navy before ending his life in France.

He was the fourth of seven children born

John Paul Jones' Cottage.

to John Paul and Jean MacDuff and his father was gardener on the estate of William Craik, the owner of Arbigland. He attended Kirkbean School, but his instincts drew him to the nearby port of Carsethorn on the Solway Firth. William Craik's son recalled that he 'would run to Carsethorn whenever his father would let him off, talk to the sailors and clamber over the ships', and that 'he taught his playmates to manoeuvre their little boats to mimic a naval battle, while he, taking his stand on the tiny cliff overlooking the roadstead, shouted shrill commands at his imaginary fleet.'

At the age of 13 he sailed south to Whitehaven on the Cumberland coast and signed up for a seven-year seaman's apprenticeship. He travelled as far away as Barbados and Virginia, where his older brother was flourishing as a tailor, and he had a brief experience on a slave ship from Whitehaven called the *King George*. It was only 50ft long, had a crew of six, carried 77 negroes and the smell could apparently be detected miles away. He quitted the ship in disgust, calling it 'an abominable trade'.

When he was only 21 he found himself acting skipper of the brig *John*, when both the captain and the mate went down with yellow fever. The Scottish owners were so impressed with his performance that they appointed him captain on a permanent basis and awarded him a percentage share of any cargoes.

He was described as being slight and wiry in body, about 5ft 5in tall with high cheekbones and a strong cleft chin. He was always neatly dressed, had an eye for the ladies and was known as a 'dandy skipper'. He also had a very short temper…one sailor died after being flogged by him and he killed another man during an alleged mutiny attempt in 1773. He survived the charges by moving to Virginia, to take over the estate of his recently-deceased brother.

The American Revolution was beginning to simmer and Jones had little sympathy with the British Government. He offered his services to the newly-formed Continental Navy and was appointed as a First Lieutenant, rapidly making a name for himself in the growing hostilities of what became known as the American War of Independence.

On 6 February France joined the war on the side of the US and Jones found himself fighting against Britain while based in the port of Brest. He formed a friendship with the American Commissioner in France and at Quiberon persuaded the French to salute the American flag – the first time it had been hoisted in a foreign harbour.

He sailed up the Irish Sea, making a nuisance of himself by capturing and destroying small vessels, and he carried out a hit and run raid on his old haunt of Whitehaven. Apparently the crew were not as enthusiastic as he was and were close to mutiny. He had not been detected, though, and his plan was to wreck the two forts that guarded the harbour. Two small boats landed at midnight in calm weather and Jones's boat spiked the cannon of one of the forts. He then went to the other one to find that the crew had gone to the pub instead. He knocked it out himself, set fire to some colliers and dragged the crew away. The inhabitants were naturally terrified by the whole thing and new guns were quickly installed. A legacy of the raid was that until fairly recently there was a dance in

John Paul Jones (original in Tullie House).

after its captain had been killed and its second in command mortally wounded.

By this time the Royal Navy was in full pursuit and a squadron of ships was sent out to capture 'the pirate'. Jones was well able to keep ahead of them, however, and his great moment came on 23 September 1779 when he was commanding the 42-gun *Bonhomme Richard*. Two Royal Navy ships were escorting a convoy of merchant vessels off Flamborough Head in Yorkshire and after a full engagement Jones's ship was clearly sinking. The British captain is said to have asked whether the *Bonhomme Richard* was surrendering when Jones gave his famous reply 'I have not yet begun to fight.'

Jones then rammed the British ship and a boarding party captured her. The French were delighted and responded by making him Chevalier Paul Jones and the Continental Congress produced a gold medal in his honour in 1787. He was now the toast of Paris and in 1781 he returned to America, where he was given a vote of thanks by Congress and was given command of the *America*, the largest ship in the US fleet. His fighting days in America were over, however, and he never finally took command of the vessel, spending the remaining years of the war advising on how the navy could be established as a professional force.

In 1788 he was in Russia serving as an admiral in the Black Sea Fleet of Empress Catherine II and earned yet more distinction. At the Battle of Liman he secretly reconnoitred the Turkish fleet in a rowing boat and later destroyed 15 of their ships, taking 1,600 prisoners.

Amazingly, he then took a brief trip to England, where he narrowly escaped being

Whitehaven called 'the Paul Jones', and when the music stopped the girls would always grab at the nearest man mimicking sheer fright.

Jones' next plan was to capture the Earl of Selkirk, who had been among those pressing charges of murder against him. He lived off the Kirkudbright coast, an area Jones knew like the back of his hand. When he found out from the head gardener that the earl was away he got ready to leave, but his crew, who had left Whitehaven empty-handed, insisted on looting the house. He allowed them to take the family silver but nothing else. At this point the butler tried to hide the silver and the countess, who had just finished breakfast, was astonished to see a group of 'horrid-looking wretches' surrounding the house. Jones was clearly embarrassed by the incident and when he heard that the countess had behaved with such poise he bought it and returned it with a letter of apology. Shortly afterwards Jones spotted HMS *Drake*, a 20-gun sloop, near Carrickfergus in Northern Ireland. The equally matched vessels fought for over an hour, with the *Drake* surrendering murdered when he landed at Harwich.

Jones retired to Paris, but his health was failing and he died on 18 July 1792 at the age of 45. For over a century his body lay pickled in alcohol in an unmarked grave reserved for foreign Protestants. It was not until the early 20th century that President Teddy Roosevelt ordered an intensive search for his body. It was discovered in 1905 and in an elaborate ceremonial it was brought back to the United States, accompanied by three cruisers. When the convoy reached Chesapeake Bay seven battleships joined the procession and the first four fired 15-gun salutes as a tribute to their champion.

Jones's body now lies in a magnificent marble sarcophagus in Annapolis Naval Academy.

KIPPFORD

Situated at the mouth of the River Urr, Kippford was once an important coastal packet port with a mill, two quarries and a

shipyard. It experienced some success, but also tragedy. In 1836 the Kippford schooner *The Dispatch* was wrecked off the coast with the loss of six local men in sight of their homes and families. Today it is a thriving yacht centre with many colourful regattas during the summer season.

KING ARTHUR

Cumbria has a claim on a British hero who, according to legend, championed the Christian cause against invading Pagans. *Rex quondam, rexque futuris*, the once and future King: Arthur.

There are dozens of places in England and Scotland that claim him for their own and anyone who comes to any firm conclusions about such a foggy period of British history is treading on dangerous ground. There is a growing and compelling case, however, despite all the smoke and mirrors for placing King Arthur and Merlin in the Border region, and in particular around Carlisle. In fact, the Cumbria Tourist Board now claims that the evidence that his real base was in this area is 'overwhelming'.

Kippford, an attractive port at the mouth of the River Urr.

Being cautious folk, the Cumbrians have always played down any attempts at romancing the past, but there is little doubt now that Arthur existed, probably as a post-Roman chieftain battling against Saxon, Irish and Pictish thrusts into the British heartlands. He made a massive impact on his time and the area is riddled with places named after him and toponymic research shows that nine of Arthur's 13 battles probably took place between the Antonine and Roman walls.

Much of the tradition and legend comes from the historic heroic poetry of the Welsh. Bards such as Taliesin, Aneirin and Lywarch Hen tell of the 'Gwyr y Gogledd' or 'The men of the North'. What must be difficult for them to accept, though, is that this in fact is the literature of the Cymric people of Cumbria, and further north before the Saxons conquered the area. Arthur is mentioned in five of the poems.

It was Sir Walter Scott who began to question the claims of Wales and Cornwall as being the centres of Arthurian action. In his introduction to *The Vision of Don Roderick*, he wrote:

'Much of the ancient poetry preserved in Wales refers less to the history of the Principality to which their name is now limited, than to events which happened in the North-West of England and the South-West of Scotland, where the Britons for a long time made a long stand against the Saxons.

'The original locality of the traditions is probably the Cumbrian region taken in its widest extent from the Firths of Clyde and

Loch Arthur possibly takes its name from King Arthur — a legacy of the Arthurian legend of the Solway.

Loch Arthur, a peaceful enigmatic place — it is easy to imagine this as the location of the legend of Excalibur...

Forth southward and westward along the borders of the Northumbrian Kingdom in which the famous exploits of the British Cymric struggle with the Northumbrian Angles became the theme of a native minstrelsy transplanted into Brittany by refugees of the Saxon conquest.'

F.J. Carruthers, in his book *People called Cumbri*, has an unusual theory about the 'sword in the stone' legend. He claims it is an allegory of the manufacture of weapons from stone, particularly rich hematite ore found in the western fells of the Lake District. Arthur would have been in contact with the sword makers who made the beautiful weapons which were in use well before the Roman invasion. The famous Embleton Sword now in the British museum is an example of the exquisite craftsmanship that went into their making. The hardness of the metal gave the Celtic resistance

a huge advantage, both over the shorter Roman stabbing sword and the more primitive swords of the Saxons. The linking of Merlin with the legend adds credence to the semi-magical status which the swordsmiths enjoyed. A modern-day parallel can be seen in the making of the Japanese Samurai swords. The forging of the weapon is an elaborate ritual and the maker is a cult figure. Apparently the process of hardening by immersion in water is mysterious and only half understood by the smith, and the climax of the whole operation is a quenching that has an almost religious significance. It also helps to explain the semi-mythical nature of the swords themselves and why perhaps the faithful Bedivere was so loathe to throw Excalibur away at the command of his dying King.

Following the Roman withdrawal from Britain in 410, political and military power in the centuries that followed centred around the southern Scotland area. Some researchers have suggested that there were a few Camelots and that Carlisle, because of its strategic defensive location, was one of them.

One of Arthur's military bases was possibly at the fort of Camboglanna, now known as Birdoswald. This is also believed to have been the location of Arthur's epic last battle, the Battle of Camlan, where he was mortally wounded.

A North American historian, the late Norma Goodrich, has written three books about Arthurian Britain and claims that Arthur, or at least his head, is buried at Arthuret church, just south of Longtown. Arthur's father, Uther Pendragon, is said to have had a castle 30 miles away at Kirby Stephen. The ruins of Pendragon Castle post-date this period but underneath it are the ruins of a much earlier one…Goodrich focusses on Carlisle because of its extensive set of Roman forts extending all the way to the Solway as well as the fact that it was a major junction point for several Roman roads.

It would appear that Carlisle was once one of the largest and newest of Rome's walled cities and that even after the collapse of their empire, royal visitors and important personages were taken on tours of 'Lordly Carlisle'. According to legend Merlin used to place the severed heads of his enemies on its walls. It was one of the strongest fortresses and military staging areas in the country, and it held out as a British redoubt long after major areas in the east had been overrun by the Saxons.

One Scottish historian, the late O.G.S. Crawford, went on many hiking expeditions along Hadrian's Wall and was quite convinced that Arthur was wounded at Camboglanna or Camlan Fort, now Birdoswald, and that his body was taken west back to his tribal heartlands. There is certainly evidence from the masses of Arthurian poetry and tradition that a great king's body was transported downriver and out to sea on a royal barge.

It is a neat theory and one that complements the romance and drama of the Solway and Border landscape itself. Whether it is all true or not will perhaps never be known, although Norma Goodrich was hopeful that one day, maybe when someone at last found *The Lost Annals of Scotland*, the truth would finally emerge.

Perhaps the last word should go to Sir Winston Churchill, who was firmly convinced that Arthur existed and referred to him as the captain who 'gathered the forces of Roman Britain'. He also added that even if he had not existed, he 'ought to have done'.

KIRKANDREWS UPON ESK CHURCH

This elegant Georgian church stands in an isolated field next to the River Esk south of Canonbie. It was built in 1776 and is the centre of a large but thinly populated parish in Cumbria. This puts it in the heart of what were once known as the Debatable Lands: the no man's land between England and Scotland and for centuries the refuge of outlaws from both sides of the Border. It has a beautiful Italianate interior dating from the 1890s and is connected to Netherby Hall, on the opposite side of the Esk, by a small suspension bridge built in 1877.

Kirkandrews Church — elegant Georgian design.

Kirkandrews Church.

Many of the weathered sandstone tombstones are now unreadable, but one of the oldest, belonging to Rosi Graham, who died in 1683, is still legible.

There are also the graves of two military men who saw action in the 1800s. The first is Lancelot Armstrong's. His obituary in the *Carlisle Patriot* read:

'February 5th 1848 at Gilnockie Cottage, Cannonbie on the 23, ult, aged 63, Lancelot Armstrong Esq. Surgeon of the Royal Navy and late of The Naval Hospital at The cape of Good Hope. The deceased served as assistant surgeon on board the Ajax at The Battle of Trafalgar. He was also on board one of the ships under Admiral Duckworth, when she blew up in the passage of the Dardanelles. He lost the whole of his clothes etc and saved his life by swimming.'

The other gravestone belongs to captain Samuel Rome of the 4th West India Regiment, whose obituary from 1824 reads:

'Captain Rome served under The Duke of Holland as a sergeant, and received his commission from the hands of the Duke, on account of his conduct in hoisting the standard of his regiment, after it had been shot away.'

KIRKCONNEL

In Kirkconnel churchyard, under the shade of a large yew tree, are the heavily worn gravestones of two 16th-century lovers. 'Fair

fishery without nets and a people without business…'

Kirkcudbright has since developed into a beautiful place, however, and has been colonised by artists since the 19th century. One of the famous 'Glasgow Boys' school, E.A. Hornel's studio is now a museum.

Gypsies were numerous along the Borders until the late 18th century and in the churchyard there is a monument to Billy Marshall – one of their 'kings' who died in 1790, apparently at the age of 120! One of his seven wives, Flora Marshall, is said to have inspired Sir Walter to cast her as the model for Meg Merrilees in his novel *Guy Mannering*.

The town jail or tollbooth once held the famous Paul Jones, charged with having caused a seaman's death. He was cleared of the charge, joined the American navy and later raided the town when he was captain of *The Ranger*.

Lochmaben Castle – traditionally thought to be the birthplace of Robert the Bruce.

LOCHMABEN CASTLE

The present overgrown ruin of Lochmaben Castle guarded the route north from England into Annandale and it changed hands at least a dozen times during the Scottish Wars of Independence. It was built by King Edward I in 1299 and contained a well-fortified building with walls 10ft thick, a tower house and an inner moat probably connected to the nearby loch.

The town had a long association with the Bruce family and local tradition has it that it was the birthplace of Robert the Bruce, but Turnberry on the Ayrshire coast has a similar claim. In 1542 King James V's Scottish army gathered here before marching to defeat by the English at the battle of Solway Moss and

in 1564 Mary Queen of Scots dined here with her new husband Lord Darnley. She and her troops were in pursuit of her half-brother, the Earl of Moray, who had taken up arms against her in protest at her marriage. He had fled south to Carlisle in hopes of gaining support from Queen Elizabeth I of England.

After the Act of Union in 1603 the castle fell into disrepair and was never again to be a place of strategic advantage.

THE LOCHMABENSTONE

This is a huge glacial erratic of historic and prehistoric interest. It stands only a few hundred yards from the Esk estuary and marked the Scottish side of the great crossing point or wath

The Clochmabenstane or the Lochmaben Stone — once the Wardens of the Marches and their associates met here on "Days of Truce".

from England. Once a staging ground for invading armies and crucial meetings between wardens and government officials from both countries, it has probably been in its present position for thousands of years.

The Lochmaben Stone is a huge glacial erratic, over six feet in height.

The stone's ancient name was 'Clochmaben' and there are various theories about its origin. Some think that it is Celtic (the chief stone of the cluster), others link it to King Arthur. Mabon was one of his knights and there are too many local references to him for the theory to be ignored. The British inhabitants of Roman Solway worshipped the god Maponus, sometimes called Mabon, and altars to him have been found at several nearby settlements. What is not in doubt, however, is that this was the site of primitive worship in the Bronze Age period and that the stone is the last remnant of an ancient circle.

THE MERKLAND CROSS

In a field next to the M74 at Kirtlebridge stands an ancient cross said to be associated with legends of the slaughter of a military commander. The Clan Maxwell record that it was put up as a memorial to John, Master of

The Merkland Cross allegedly marks the place where John Maxwell met his death.

Maxwell, who was killed there on 22 July 1484.

His father Robert was Lord Maxwell, who, though elderly, was still in possession of the family estates and titles. John was his junior, even though he was in his 50s and had sired 10 children. He was the Steward of Annandale and it was his responsibility to administer justice on behalf of the King of Scotland.

Two outlawed Scots – Alexander, Duke of Albany, and James, Earl of Douglas – crossed the Border with 500 heading for Lochmaben. It was market day and most of the country folk were in town and they knew that their farms would be undefended. At first they caused havoc, but a reinforcement of royal troops arrived and began to force the raiders away, pushing them back across the River Annan and its tributaries, the Water of Milk and the Mein Water.

At some point in the battle the Master of Maxwell joined in with his men but he was wounded and had to dismount. While he was watching the end of the affray he was stabbed in the back and died before anyone could help him.

NEW ABBEY CORNMILL

Built in the 1700s, the cornmill occupies the site of a much older mill built by the monks of Sweetheart Abbey 500 years earlier. The millpond and the one kilometre long Lade serving it were probably also built by the monks. Unusually the working mill also combined a house for the miller and his family. In those days, because of the need to dry the corn, there was always a risk of fire and the living house would have been a separate building.

Just beyond the mill is the New Mill Pow, a small river that also once drove a

snuff mill and a saw mill. The river was one of the reasons for the establishment of the abbey and for many centuries it was used by small boats able to navigate almost as far as the village itself.

ORCHARDTON TOWER

Orchardton Tower is situated a few miles south of the town of Dalbeattie, just off the main A711 road. The tower is circular and is the only one of its kind in Scotland, although a few examples are to be found in Ireland. Orchardton has a vaulted basement with a small access door, but the main entrance is by a flight of stone steps to what is effectively the first floor. Originally there were two upper floors in the building, but these have now gone, although it is still possible to climb the full 33ft of the building to the wall walk by means of a spiral staircase set into the wall. The outbuildings, which are now in ruins, would probably have been two storeys high, with a kitchen and possibly a hall for the lord on the first floor.

The tower was originally built in 1456 by John Cairns, who held the prestigious position of collector of customs for Linlithgow. It stayed in his family for almost 100 years until there was a lengthy dispute over a legacy and the estate and the tower were passed to the crown.

In 1615 the estate was purchased by Sir Robert Maxwell, who became the 1st Baronet of Orchardton. The Sir Robert Maxwell who was the owner in 1745 (the Maxwells didn't seem to use a lot of imagination or go for much variation when choosing Christian names – most of them were called Robert!) was wounded in the Battle of Culloden. He was taken prisoner and sent to Carlisle for execution; however, he held a commission in the French army and this saved his life – he was treated as a prisoner of war and sent to France. On his return to Orchardton his story provided the inspiration for Sir Walter Scott and his novel *Guy Mannering*.

The Maxwells lived in Orchardton until 1765 when the 7th Baronet stared work on a

Opposite: New Abbey Corn Mill dates from the 1700's.

Orchardton is the only circular tower house in Scotland.

The dark interior of Robert the Bruce's Cave.

magnificent new house; the venture bankrupted him and he was forced to sell Orchardton to James Douglas, a Liverpool merchant.

ROBERT THE BRUCE CAVE

Born at Lochmaben Catel in 1274, Robert the Bruce was crowned King of Scotland in 1306. The dates are not quite clear, but after suffering a defeat, possibly at the hands of the Lord of Lorn at a battle in Strath-Fillan in 1306, he was a hunted man. His sister had been captured and three of his brothers executed by the English army.

For three months he hid in a cave and this one at Kirkpatrick Fleming is one of the places that he could have hidden in. Other caves that claim the honour are in Rathlin Island in Northern Ireland and Drumadoon on the Isle of Arran.

The story goes that while idling the time away Bruce noticed a spider building a web in the cave's entrance. The spider fell down time after time, but finally succeeded. It is only a legend, but apparently this so inspired him that he vowed to continue the struggle of independence against the English. In 1314, against considerable odds, he won the Battle of Bannockburn, established his claim to the throne of Scotland and began the process of freeing the country.

A mysterious carving beside near entrance to the cave.

The cave consists of a small chamber about 12ft in diameter that has been carved out of the red sandstone cliff about 30 feet above the River Kirtle. It can be reached only by being lowered on a rope over the overhang and swinging into the cave. Because of many accidents caused by people trying to reach it the local council decided to build the present

Opposite: Robert the Bruce's Cave, Kirkpatrick Fleming.

footpath to it.

Recently the Bruce family has favoured the location of the cave as being in Rathlin Island, but this one has a strong claim as some versions of the legend talk of Sir William Irving, a local landowner, having helped Bruce to hide here.

Nearby is Bonshaw Tower, with its eight-foot thick walls. It was one of the strongholds of the Irving family, who owned the valley from 900 when the tower was built. They also had seven minor fortresses up and down the river, known as the Seven Irving Towers, and some of the remains of these are still visible. The family has a long and distinguished history. They supported and possibly protected Bruce when he was on the run from

the English and during the two world wars they were prominent officers in both the army and navy. One of them commanded the *Queen Mary*.

THE RUTHWELL CROSS

This magnificent artistic treasure stands in a small church in the town of Ruthwell, just a few miles south of Dumfries. Scholars maintain that it is the most important sculptural survival from Anglo-Saxon Britain and even from early mediaeval Europe.

Originally the Angles had been pagans worshipping Odin and Thor, but in AD635 Oswald and his brother Oswui, returning from exile at the monastery on the Isle of Iona, reclaimed their kingdom and brought Gaelic missionaries with them. The Angles became converts and began extending their power westwards to the Solway and the rich trading routes of the Irish sea. It was Oswui who energised this expansion, pushing further into Galloway in the mid-seventh century.

The Ruthwell cross is a symbol of his power and Christian faith. Standing 5.2 metres tall, it is carved with a mixture of sophisticated text and artistic skill and was probably intended as a preaching aid, a literal 'sermon in a stone'. It was also carefully situated well away from the highway and remote from the seaboard so that it would not be vandalised by invading barbarians.

The pictures or carvings would have been intended for the uneducated humble, who would have recognised the essential message of the Gospels. Christ's divinity, the Holy Trinity and the four Evangelists – Matthew, Mark, Luke and John – are clearly illustrated. The Latin inscriptions would probably have been for the use of the monks – the only people who would have had a classical education. There is another set of inscriptions which have been carved in runes, used by Germanic people like the Angles and Vikings. These are fragmentary quotations from one of the oldest English

The Ruthwell Cross is one of the finest and most important examples of a Anglo-Saxon Cross in Britain.

Ruthwell Church.

poems ever written called *The Dream of the Rood*. 'Rood' refers to 'cross', as in Holyrood in Edinburgh.

Runes are a form of writing which have their origin in the Greek alphabet, and it was a famous Anglo-Saxon scholar called John Mitchell Kemble who first deciphered the Ruthwell runes in the 19th century. He discovered a powerful piece of writing…

'Then the young warrior prepared himself – it was God almighty, resolute and strong; brave in the sight of many. He went up to the lofty cross, to save mankind. They pierced me with dark nails: you see the wounds, the open gashes: I durst harm none of them. They scorned us both together. Stained was I with blood that streamed…'

In the late seventh century there was a new devotional cult emerging out of the Mediterranean, centred around the Holy Cross, and the runes could possibly have been intended for those with no knowledge of Latin. Such was the strength of the oral tradition of the day that they probably knew the poem by heart.

The cross itself has had a violent history. In earlier times it would have stood exposed to the wind and rain. In 1664 it was to be pulled down and smashed on the instructions of the General Assembly of The Church of Scotland. The Assembly, convened at Aberdeen on 28 July 1640, passed an 'Act anant the demolishing of Idolatrous monuments'.

Happily, the then parish minister of Ruthwell, the Revd Gavin Young, paid no attention to the Act and instead tried as carefully as he could to dismantle the cross and hide it underground in the churchyard until the religious mania had passed.

In the 18th century pieces of the cross were moved into the church and in the early 19th century the process of reconstruction was begun under the direction of Dr Duncan (priest at Ruthwell 1799–1843). Sadly, some mistakes were made and the cross is not quite in its original state. Finally it was re-erected in the manse garden and in 1877 it was moved to its special place inside the church.

The Revd Gavin Young is very much worth mentioning. He was the minister at Ruthwell during the turbulent years of 1617–71, when religious fanatics of all denominations were harrying dissenters throughout Scotland. It was a dangerous time but it is reported in the *Picture of Scotland* (third edition of 1834) that he was 'more concerned about the spirit of religion than its forms'. He protected the cross from the zealots who wanted to destroy it and treated the Presbyterians, Episcopalians and Covenantors with equal courtesy and disregard.

'He had a fair word to everyone, and in secret made the church and living at Ruthwell the chief object of his care. He maintained his character, was respected by all parties for his moderation and learning; lived a tranquil and useful life; and died in peace, after enjoying his cure for 54 years.' Quite an epitaph…

SAVINGS BANK MUSEUM

In 1810 Dr Henry Duncan, the aforementioned Minister of Ruthwell Church, opened the world's first savings bank, enabling local people to receive interest on their modest savings. The museum, in an 18th-century cottage, has collections of early savings boxes, coins and banknotes from all over the world.

Dr Duncan was no ordinary minister. He

The Savings Bank Museum, Ruthwell.

was born near Dumfries in 1774 and when first appointed he did all in his power to alleviate the near starvation conditions of his parishioners. He restored the magnificent Ruthwell Cross, founded a newspaper, wrote tracts and papers on slave emancipation and education and presented the first paper on fossil footprints to the Royal Society of Edinburgh in 1828. His passion for science and geology had led to the discovery of fossil footprints in Cornockle Quarry near Lochmaben. Interestingly, his discoveries did not seem to conflict with his religious beliefs and in this sense he was years ahead of his time.

SIR WALTER SCOTT

In a previous century Walter Scott could have been as hardy a Reiver as any of his ancestors. Although lamed by polio in childhood he grew up to be a sturdy six-footer of great physical endurance, but instead of rustling cattle for a living he started searching for the old legends, incomparable ballads and daring deeds that would reappear in his novels and poems.

Until he cast his spell, his contemporaries' perception of the Borderlands was that they were nothing but barbaric wastelands, unfit for civilised people to be seen in. When he

Sir Walter Scott, (original in Tullie House).

Sir Walter Scott married Charlotte Carpenter in Carlisle Cathedral.

died they were seen for what they really were: places of haunting beauty where genuine heroism ran alongside cruelty and crime. He has often been accused of romanticising the place, but in Scott's world there was more than just idealised confection. There was sugar but there was also the salt of realism. Fairies, gallantries and heroines were there, but so were the murderers and the dogs of war.

Scott was born on 15 August 1771 in Edinburgh, the son of Walter, a solicitor, and Anne, a daughter of a professor of medicine. Scott was at Edinburgh High School and the University, where he studied art and law. He then qualified as a barrister, but his instincts drew him south to the Borderlands; by the age of 21 he was spending his leisure time tramping the haunts of the Reivers and listening to the old stories, feeding his passion for Scottish history. He particularly remembered wandering around the walls and gates of Carlisle, where he had seen the spikes

which had secured the heads of the rebels executed in the 1745 rebellion.

Scott was a frequent visitor to the Solway and in 1797 he was on a riding holiday in the Lake District when he met a 17-year-old French girl called Charlotte Carpenter. She was a Charpentier from Lyon, but her parents had died and she was under the guardianship

The Solway Firth — a dramatic description can be found in Scott's novel, Red Gauntlet.

of Lord Devonshire at the time. Why she was in Carlisle and what the circumstances of her background were remains a mystery, but Scott, 'on the rebound' from an earlier failed romance, was enchanted. It was love at first sight and he reputedly proposed to her at the 'popping stone' at Gilsland near Brampton. On Christmas Eve of the same year they were married in Carlisle Cathedral and they remained together for 29 years, producing five children. Sadly, Charlotte died in 1826 at the age of 46 and Scott was devastated. To make matters worse, his printing business would soon collapse and he would be massively in debt. After her death there was a poignant cameo written by his daughter Anne on a visit to Carlisle with her father in 1828.

'Papa took me with him to the Cathedral. This he had often done before; but he said he must stand once more on the spot where he married poor Mama.'

Scott was now writing in deadly earnest to pay off his creditors. Although he was already a hugely successful novelist, he could not afford not to work and his output was prodigious, with many of his stories centred around the Solway.

He was in touch with a man called Joseph Train, a customs officer who spent most of his life in Castle Douglas. His passion was antiquarian research and he had promised to send Scott anything of interest. One day he sent to Abbotsford, Scott's home, notes he had made on two local characters. The first one was about Isobel Walker, who had been condemned to death in Dumfries for the concealment of the birth and murder of her baby.

It was the concealment that was the capital charge and if her sister Helen had been prepared to commit perjury by saying that she had been informed of the birth then Isobel's life would have been saved. However, Helen's firm Presbyterian conscience would not allow her to tell a lie in court and Isobel was sentenced to be hanged. Full of remorse, Helen decided to seek help. She could not afford coach travel so she walked all the way to London, a distance of about 350 miles, taking two weeks to get there. She petitioned the Duke of Argyll on behalf of her sister and he was so moved by her story that he was able to use his influence to obtain a reprieve. On leaving prison Isobel married the man who had seduced her and they lived happily in Whitehaven for the next 30 years. Helen remained a single, hard-working, respected woman in her home parish of Kirkpatrick Irongray. Isobel became the inspiration for 'Effie Deans', one of Scott's most famous heroines in *The Heart of Midlothian*, and Helen

The Dornock to Bowness Wath in winter – where Darsie Latimer attempted his ill fated crossing in Scott's novel, Red Gauntlet.

Opposite: Shadows in the north aisle — Sweetheart Abbey.

became 'Jennie Deans'.

Another extraordinary character was Robert Paterson, a stone engraver from the parish of Balmaclellan, who became 'Old Mortality' in the novel of the same name. He was famous for riding around Galloway, Ayrshire and Dumfriesshire on a white horse looking for the graves of Covenanters slain during 'the killing times'. His self-appointed mission in life was to repair and restore these graves. If he found that there were no inscriptions he would carve one himself on to the stones.

Finally there is a dramatic scene in *Redgauntlet* where Darsie Latimer, travelling from Edinburgh to England in search of his family, mistimes his crossing of the Solway from Dornock to Bowness. The tide is coming in and he is sinking in quicksand. He is rescued by Redgauntlet, a local aristocrat who has been fishing for salmon on horseback. The warning that he gives Darsie has often been quoted.

'He that dreams on the Solway may wake in the next world…'

Some critics claim that Scott's knowledge of Scotland and his ability to resurrect the old stories and dying legends created a romantic image of Scotland that had little basis in reality. While his style of writing now seems ponderous and the dialogue too dense with local dialect for modern ears, there is no doubt that his understanding, sympathy and imagination did not distort but actually enhanced the truth. As George Macdonald Fraser observed, 'He was the greatest man the region ever produced.'

SWEETHEART ABBEY

This was once called New Abbey, but the Cistercian monks renamed it 'Dulce Cor' or Sweetheart Abbey, in recognition of its founder Lady Devorgilla. She was a lady of the royal blood of Scotland and had signed a charter establishing the abbey on 10 April

Sweetheart Abbey from the graveyard.

Overleaf: The nave and aisles, Sweetheart Abbey.

1273. Her beloved husband, John Balliol, had died four years earlier and she had his heart embalmed. She carried it around with her in a casket of ivory bound with enamelled silver until her own death in 1289. The casket is buried with her in the sanctuary of the monastery church. As an act of atonement to Edward I, her husband had established Balliol College in Oxford and she confirmed and endowed it in 1282.

The Cistercians, or 'the white monks', had chosen the site for their monastery well. Nestling under the protection of Criffel and with easy access to the Solway via the River Nith, it prospered. Sheep, horses, cattle and fishing were the main industries, underpinned by the rigorous discipline of daily prayer and worship. Unfortunately they hadn't anticipated the wars between England and Scotland that were to dominate the next 300 years and by the 1400s the abbey was impoverished.

As the maelstrom of the Reformation approached the monks looked to Lord Maxwell for protection, a devout Catholic who proved to be a staunch friend. In 1590 the Lords of the Congregation ordered him to destroy the buildings and he bravely refused, declaring that he was attached to the place 'quhair he was maist part brocht up in his youth.' With his help the last abbot, Gilbert Broun, continued to reside at Sweetheart and to practise the ancient faith in defiance of the new order.

In 1603 Abbot Gilbert was imprisoned in Blackness Castle for his stance, but by 1608 he was back in open defiance of his king, James VI. An attempt to arrest him was made by the Dumfries guard but they were beaten off by 'a convocation of a great number of rude and ignorant people, armed with stones, muskets and hagbuts in a tumultuous and unseemlie manner.' He eventually died in France in 1612 but not before a collection of his 'Popish copes, chalices, pictures and images and other such Popish trash' were publicly burned in Dumfries High Street.

Large sections of the abbey were then dismantled to provide stone for buildings in the village but in 1779 some far-sighted locals clubbed together to preserve the shell of the abbey church and what was left, as they were 'desirous of preserving the remainder of that building as an ornament to that part of the country'. In 1928 their successors entrusted the enchanting ruin into state care and it is now looked after by Historic Scotland.

THOMAS CARLYLE

It is doubtful if he is much read today, but in Victorian times Thomas Carlyle was hugely influential and famous for his deep, thoughtful books on history and philosophy. He was born in Ecclefechan on 4 December 1795, the eldest of nine children, and was brought up in a strict Calvinist atmosphere, where the emphasis was on frugality and discipline. He was a pupil at Annan Academy, where he showed an early promise in mathematics and then won a place at Edinburgh University to study Divinity, walking the 80-mile journey there in three days.

His parents expected him to become a preacher, but he lost his faith in traditional Christianity at the university, while at the same time keeping his belief in its values. This tension and uncertainty of outlook struck a chord with many Victorians who

'He that dreams on the Solway may wake in the next world...'
Sir Walter Scott

The Solway Firth is a dangerous, mysterious
and enigmatic shifting half-landscape.

Both Sides of the Solway

THE BATTLE OF SOLWAY MOSS, 1542

When James V of Scotland refused to join his uncle Henry VIII in rejecting the Catholic Church, Henry sent an army north on a massive raid. Incensed, James authorised Lord Maxwell, Warden of the Scottish West March, to raise an army and retaliate.

In the early hours of 24 November 1542 an army of 15,000–18,000 Scots advanced south from Langholm and crossed the River Esk at Longtown. James didn't entirely trust Maxwell and decided that he himself would lead the army, but he fell sick and got no further than Lochmaben.

The commander of the English West March was Lord Wharton, an experienced and very able soldier. He had at his disposal 3,000 men or 'lances', and a highly mobile force of 500 horses under his deputy William Musgrave. He could have stayed safely in Carlisle Castle and prepared for a siege, but he went out to meet them at Solway Moss, between Longtown and Arthuret Church. It was early dawn and he could already see the red horizon to the north where the Scots were burning the Grahams out of the Debatable Land. He chose his ground well. He positioned his main force on Arthuret Knowes, itself on a raised platform above the Esk with a clear view of the oncoming force, and he waited for them to cross the river, when they would be at their most vulnerable.

Musgrave was ordered to harass the flanks of the Scottish army, which he did to such an effect that the first signs of panic set in. He made lightning raids on their vanguard and then quickly withdrew. There was already a power struggle going on in the heart of the Scottish army with Sir John Sinclair declaring himself to be the king's favourite and therefore the leader, but the other commanders refused to accept his authority and bickered among themselves.

Solway Moss from Arthuret Church Yard.

Solway Moss was once a dangerous area with secret paths and ancient ways...

With no clear or decisive commands, the army remained immobile while Musgrave continued to attack. To their horror the Scottish commanders began to see their entire army waver and collapse. They headed north-west, back across the Esk and on to the treacherous edges of the Solway estuary and the swampy Moss. Perhaps the memory of the disaster at Flodden 19 years before was also playing on the Scots' minds, but there was complete chaos as Wharton gave brief chase. According to the official reports, four or five Scots were surrendering to a single English rider.

The remnants of the Scottish army, escaping north, found themselves set upon by the Reivers from Liddlesdale, ever keen to plunder anything that came their way regardless of nationality. Those who escaped with their lives were stripped and turned loose in their hose.

Wharton's force was too small to undertake serious pursuit, but he noted that it was good 'to hear of the spoil and taking of prisoners that night in Scotland by the Annerdales, Eskdales, Ewesdales, Wauchopdales and some of the Liddesdales.'

To King James it was a death blow. In the space of 20 years Scotland had suffered two mortal blows to its nationhood. Over a thousand Scots were made prisoners, including Sir John Sinclair and Lord Maxwell, and several hundred were killed. James had already suffered the loss of two sons and his mother, the English Princess Margaret, in the previous year, and during the next few months he wandered listlessly

...but is now crossed now by long straight roads and tracks.

from one royal residence to another. The humiliation proved too much to bear and he died at Falkland Palace at the age of 30, two weeks after the battle. Before he died he received the news that his queen had given birth to a baby girl, 'a very weak child and not like to live'. How wrong they were…this was the future Mary Queen of Scots.

THE BATTLE OF THE SARK

The Scottish War of Independence dragged on into the 15th century and the Battle of Sark, sometimes referred to as the Battle of Lochmabenstone, was fought in October 1448.

The English, despite their reputation for winning victory after victory using their formidable longbows, were defeated.

Provocation was a way of life on the Border, and harnessing the testosterone-fuelled Henry Percy, son of the Earl of Northumberland, was not easy. He destroyed the port of Dunbar in 1448 and a month later the Earl of Salisbury, Lord Warden of the March, pillaged Dumfries. These were fairly standard acts of aggression by themselves and they were not going to provoke all-out war between the two countries, but they were too much for William Douglas, the most powerful figure in the Scottish Marches. Together with his kinsmen, the Earls of Ormond, Angus and Orkney, he ransacked the Percy fiefdoms of Alwick and Warkworth in revenge. He didn't stop there and continued rampaging all over Northumberland and Cumberland.

The situation was deemed serious enough to bring King Henry VI north, but he had little stomach for a fight himself and he authorised Percy to launch a major raid on Scotland.

Percy didn't need to be asked twice, and in

The Sark Bridge crosses the border between England and Scotland.

The Battle of the Sark was fought on the dangerous Solway tidal flats.

October he gathered together an army of 6,000 men. He was accompanied by his son, Sir John Pennington, Sir Thomas Harrington and a colourful mercenary called Magnus Redmayne. They were full of confidence and as soon as they had crossed the Sark they pitched camp at Gretna. This was a disastrous choice of ground as they were positioned between the Sark and the Kirtle Water, with the highly-dangerous Solway tidal flats behind them. Effectively they were already in a vice-like trap.

The Scots had been well aware of Percy's intentions and had organised their own force, mainly made up from the men of Nithsdale and Annandale. Hugh, Earl of Ormond, a brother of the Earl of Douglas, was joined by Sir John Wallace of Craigie, the Sheriff of Ayr, Herbert Maxwell of Caerlaverock and other Border notables, totalling about 4,000 men. On 23 October they marched towards Gretna.

Percy was astonished at what he saw coming towards him, as he was totally unaware that there were any Scottish forces in the area capable of resisting him. He rapidly organised his men into their battle divisions, placing the deadly longbowmen on his left on the banks of the Kirtle Water and under the command of Sir John Pennington. He placed himself at the centre and the right wing was commanded by Redmayne. What he didn't notice was that at his rear the marshes and mud flats of the Solway were beginning to fill up. The tide was coming in…

Ormond arranged his army accordingly, placing himself at the centre opposite Percy, his left under Craigie and the right under the joint command of Maxwell and the Laird of Johnstone, the ancestor of the Johnstones of Annandale. Interestingly, these two families were later to become bitter enemies.

The Scots prepared themselves for a very nasty shower. The English longbow was one of the most lethal weapons in history, with a killing range of over 200 yards. The six-foot longbow required immensely strong arms to 'pull' it, but a practised archer could unleash 12 shots a minute. They did not aim, they fired into the air in the general direction of

The tidal flats of the Solway Firth between Old Graitney and the Lochmaben Stone — the highly prized turf was used on the Centre Court of Wimbledon and Wembley Stadium.

the enemy and waited for the infantry to wade into the resulting chaos.

At first it appeared that the battle was going to be a repeat of previous Scottish disasters, but Percy had had little time to ensure that his archers were supported by spearmen or cavalry.

The Scots' favourite weapon was the spear or lance. These were sometimes over 13 feet long and expert handlers could quickly cause panic among the enemy. There were shorter versions which could be used for throwing or thrusting, and the local Reivers were highly adept in using them. Camden and Sir Walter Scott describe Borderers on horseback spearing salmon with a spear or leister, an astonishing skill.

Wallace of Craigie spotted the weakness in the English formation immediately and ordered his spearmen to make an immediate charge. They scythed into Redmayne's division and a Scottish chronicler wrote a vivid account of what happened next.

'...his men wes sa inraget and ruscit sa furieouslie upon the Inglisch with exes, speris and halberts and maid sa great slaughter at the first to coming that they put the Inglisch men cleane aback fre thair standard and compelld thame at last to tak to flight.'

Redmayne's division was completely routed and the rest of the Scots army, sensing growing panic in the English ranks, rushed forward to join in. Percy's army was being pushed slowly back towards the fast flowing Solway channels...the chronicler continues:

'...the filling of the sea, caused many to lose their lyves and perish in the waters. Others, siean this, doubted quhidder they would fight and die with honour, or live with shame, and preferring the one to the other,

were cruellie slain upon the water bankis.'

The chronicler records that 1,500 Englishmen were killed and a further 500 drowned in trying to flee across the Solway. Pennington and Percy were taken prisoner along with dozens of other nobles. The Scots losses were estimated at around 300 men, but Wallace of Craigie, who had inspired the victory, was mortally wounded and died shortly afterwards.

For some reason the Battle of the Sark is hard to find in the history books, even though it was an important landmark in the Border story. It was a significant Scottish victory and helped them hold the initiative against an opponent distracted by foreign and then civil wars. It also raised the prestige of the Douglas clan, which the Scottish government took nervous notice of.

THE BORDER BALLADS

Would the Kray twins or Al Capone have had poems or ballads sung about them? Probably not, but the Reivers did. It seems paradoxical that a violent and brutalised people could produce poetry of such range and feeling. There were hundreds of them and many were rescued from oblivion by Sir Walter Scott, who travelled around the Borders extensively collecting as many as he could, either directly from singers or from neighbouring Borderers like William Laidlaw, James Hogg and John Leyden. He had a theory that the wilder the society the more likely the impulse towards poetry and music, and the area was fertile ground for both.

Even today the ballads have a strange and haunting power. Their themes are joy, superstition, savagery, love, incest, revenge and grief, and they relate with uncompromising directness the real story of a frontier community staring the death angel straight in the eye. Despite some flashes of wit and humour the endings are usually tragic and true to ancient tradition they were rarely written down, but handed by word of mouth and repetition to each generation.

Here is young Sandy Armstrong of Rowanburn on the eve his execution:
'O this night is my departing night, for here no longer may I stay,
There's neither friend nor foe of mine, but wishes me away.
What I have done through lack of wit, I never can recall
I hope you are all my friends as yet, goodnight and joy be with you all.'

Although they are now seen as literature, they were meant to be sung and probably much of their magic has disappeared with the music. Scott was famously criticised by an Ettrick shepherd's mother for forgetting this.

'There was never ane o' my songs prentit till ye prentit them
yoursel', and ye hae spoilt them altogether. They were made for
singin' and no' for reading, but ye hae broken the charm now, and
they'll never be sung mair.'

They must have sounded superb when they were sung. The opening lines of *Jock O' the Side* are fizzing with energy, even without the music.

'Now Liddlesadale has ridden a raid,
But I wat they had better hae stayed at hame;
For Michael o' Winfield he is dead,
And Jock O' the side is prisoner ta'en.
For Mangerton house lady Downie has gane,
Her coats she has kilted up to the knee;
And down the water wi' sped she runs
While tears in spaits fall fast frae her eye.'

The narrative races on. Three Amstrong men are chosen to rescue Jock from Newcastle prison. They ride with reversed shoes on their horses to confuse any chasing group, cut down trees at Chollerford to help them scale the walls and without any scruple kill a porter at the gates of the city.

A Border Tower near the Merkland Cross - towers were always built on a good vantage point.

'His neck in twa the Armstrongs wrang;
Wi foot or hand he ne'er played pa!
His life and keys at once they hae tae'en
And cast his body ahind the wall.'

Of course, Jock is rescued and the Armstrongs ride back in triumph to Liddlesdale. The ballad is typical in that even though the violence is shocking it is not dwelled upon and is almost an incidental in the story.

Folk music revivals in the last few years have helped to regenerate interest and songs such as *The Unquiet Grave, Jock O' Hazeldean* and *The Bonny Lass O' Fyvie*, though not Border Ballads, can give some clue as to their beauty and resonance.

Some of the better known ones around the Solway area were *The Ballad of Kinmont Willie, Helen of Kirkonnel, Jock O' the Side, Hughie the Graeme* and *Johnnie Armstrong*. Even in that small selection there is evidence that the ballads did not only celebrate battles and daring raids, but also that love was also a recurring theme. *The Border Widow's Lament* has a heart-rending simplicity and unsentimental directness. The woman's husband has just been killed and:

'I sewed his sheet marking my name, I washed his corpse myself alane,
I watched his body night and day, nae living creature came that way.
I took his body on my back, and whiles I pray and whiles I sat,
I digged a grave and laid him in, and covered him wi' grass sae green.
But think nae ye my heart was sair, when I laid the clay on his yellow hair,
Oh think nae ye my heart was awae, when I turned about and went away,
No living man I'll love again.'

In his memoirs, Thomas Bewick, the famous engraver, tells how during his childhood the winter evenings were spent listening to the traditional tales of daring deeds and brave young lovers. They were not about gangsters, murder and burnings all the time. There were good landlords, kind neighbours, spontaneous generosities and bold, independent, honest people. He remembers that he was enthralled by them and 'was greatly distressed, and often gave vent to tears'.

The ballads seemed to spontaneously arise from the land itself. There are no authors protecting copyright and they were never written down, but passed from generation to generation by word of mouth. In many ways the Border Reivers could have been just carrrying on from where their Anglo-Saxon and Viking ancestors left off. These old warriors liked nothing better than to while away the long winter nights with poems glorifying war, raiding and revenge, and they would have had their own bards, highly respected members of their communities with vast memories packed with genealogies and history, to inspire and entertain them. They sound like cosy evenings, but there was danger flickering in the fire-lit shadows as well. These were prickly people, sensitive to the slightest criticism of their honour and bravery, and they would take deadly revenge at the slightest offence. The bards themselves were aware of this, but even the warriors would be wary of crossing them, as a nickname or character assassination in just one line in a ballad would reverberate for generations. They seemed to lead a mystical, shaman-like existence – of the community but somehow separate from it. Often when singing from memory they would disappear into a trancelike state.

Sir Walter Scott might have met one of the last of them. When he was only 21 he was visiting Liddlesdale one spring 'in blirting, snawy weather' collecting folk stories and ballads with a fellow Borderer, J.E. Shortreed.

They were trying to find a man called 'auld Jonathan Graham, the lang Quaker', who held a vast repository of ballads in his 80-year-old head. Shortreed recalls:

'I'll never forget his apperance, tall and sae thin as to be more of a walking skeleton than a living being. Indeed ye wadna hae said to look at him that he was a human being, till he began to recite and then fired up he got prodigiously animated. He spoke, or rather "skraughed", in a loud stentorian voice, which formed the oddest contrast imaginable with his worn and emaciated figure.'

He paused for a while, Scott gave him generous amounts of brandy and he fainted, so they carried him out into the fresh air and threw water onto his face until he revived. Then he was off 'roaring the outlandish lilt again. He made the awfuest and uncoest howling sound I ever heard. It was a mixture of a sort of horrible and eldritch cries, and to have looked at him you would have thought it impossible they would come out of that dead trunk.'

They eventually put the man to bed. Whether his recital style was typical is another question, but the performance was dramatic enough in itself to testify to the depths that the ballads could reach in the collective folk memory.

It was the famous Northumbrian historian George M. Trevelyan who captured their beauty and timeless, essential nature when he wrote:

'They were cruel, coarse savages, slaying each other like the beasts of the forest; and yet they were also poets who could express in the grand style the inexorable fate of the indidvidual man and woman, the infinite pity for all cruel things which they none the less perpetually inflicted upon one another. It was not one ballad-maker alone but the whole cut-throat population who felt this magnanimous sorrow and the consoling charms of the highest poetry. The songs on both sides of the Cheviot ridge were handed down by oral tradition among the shepherds and among the farm girls who, for centuries, sang them to each other at the milking. If the people had not loved the songs many of the best would have perished. The Border ballads, for good or evil, express this society and its quality of mind.'

THE BORDER REIVERS

It was Edward I who lit the fuse. In 1286 he launched a brutal invasion of Scotland, massacring almost the entire population of Berwick in the process.

For the next 300 years the dogs of war ran

The Tullie House Museum has an excellent multi media presentation capturing the lives of the Border Reivers.

A reivers 'Steill Bonnet' and breastplate, Tullie House Museum.

riot in the Borders and it wasn't until the Act of Union in 1601 that they were stilled.

A ferocious cycle of revenge, retribution, raid and counter-raid swirled among the valleys and moors as the rule of law was abandoned. Governments encouraged the Borderers to harass across the frontiers and the area was turned into a charred wilderness. When they were not fighting for their countries they were brawling with each other, plundering in any direction, with a fine disregard for robbing from their own neighbours. Cattle rustling, feuding, murder, kidnapping, arson and pillaging were part of everyday life. These were the Border Reivers, the wild men of the north who have come down to us in the legendary Border Ballads.

They have been romanticised and vilified; characterised as proud, gallant, independent rascals or stone-hearted killers, they left the English language with two chilling words, 'bereaved' and 'blackmail'.

In a way, their appearance was inevitable. They occupied a buffer zone between two of the most quarrelsome nations in Europe and they never really knew whose side they were meant to be on. A modern equivalent might be the ungovernable mountains between Afghanistan and Pakistan, where lip service is paid to the rule of law and loyalty is bought by the highest bidder. The Reivers would have been perfectly at home there.

Can they really be blamed? Threatened on both sides, they turned to violence firstly as a means of self-preservation and secondly to make a living. The continual wars had left them with very little wealth and they cherished allegiance to their own families as they were the only people they could trust. The arbitrary England–Scotland border was

to them a puzzling artifice, which bore no relation to their ancestral memory. They had once been united in the kingdoms of Rheged and Northumbria, which had straddled vast areas of northern Britain. No wonder their loyalties were fickle.

Eventually the conditions under which they were forced to live led to destitution, which in turn increased the violence. Nobody and nothing was safe and it got worse and worse. Shaped by ordeals that passed the rest of Britain by, robbery and extortion became a virtual profession.

THE DEBATABLE LANDS

One of the strategies which both governments tried to use was the division of the Borders into 'Marches', three in Scotland and three in England, each controlled by a warden. While this was fine in theory, it seldom worked in practice, mainly because the wardens were neck high in extortion and intrigue themselves.

The most notorious area was a stretch of boggy land near the Esk basin north of Carlisle, where powerful families like the Grahams, Elliots, Armstrongs and Bells were impossible to police and the wardens left them well alone. Eventually, both London and Edinburgh had had enough of them and the area was divided into two by a man-made ditch called the Scots Dyke. The western, or English, side was given to the Grahams and Bells and the eastern, or Scottish, side to the Armstrongs and Elliots.

It is said that the word 'blackmail' was invented by the Grahams of Arthuret. Hutcheon Graham, a local ruffian, would

collect money each week after Sunday Evensong in the church porch. If people failed to pay up they were liable to have their cattle stolen. It was basically protection money and originally it was a payment of grain or 'meale', which would be handed over at night or in the 'black'. Interestingly, there is still a custom in the Borders' cattle and sheep markets of the seller handing over 'luck' money to the buyer. It's a sort of 'thanks for buying' but is also probably a legacy of the protection system.

CHRISTIANITY

Three giants of the early church in Britain, St Ninian, St Patrick and St Kentigern, did much to both establish and nourish the Christian faith in the Solway region, then part of the ancient kingdom of Rheged. The Romans had certainly allowed Christian worship before they withdrew in the fourth century, but it is St Ninian who is credited with evangelising southern Scotland – building its first church at Whithorn in Galloway.

There is debate about Ninian's exact birthplace, but it is thought to have been somewhere in the Solway region in about AD350, and his parents were fortunate enough to be able to send him to Rome to be educated. His abilities were noticed by successive popes, and he was made a bishop and commissioned to return to Britain to preach the Catholic faith. He built Whithorn in around AD397, making it the first Christian settlement north of Hadrian's Wall, and he and his monks set about travelling throughout Scotland preaching the Gospels. He is often referred to as the apostle of the

northern Britons and Picts and was known for his miracles, reputedly curing a chieftain of blindness. Today there are churches all over Scotland and northern England which are named after him. The cathedral which was built to house his remains is now in ruins, but pilgrims still make the journey to the windswept little peninsula at Whithorn, and they also visit the cave on the seashore nearby where he used to retire to meditate and pray.

Then came St Patrick. Again there is doubt about the exact whereabouts of his birth, but one recent author has pinpointed it as being near Greenhead, between Haltwhistle and Brampton, in about 415.

He wrote two books, which have astonishingly survived, and in one of them, *The Confessio*, a sort of autobiography, he relates that when he was younger he took little interest in Christianity until he was kidnapped at the age of 15 by Irish raiders, who shipped him to Ulster to work as a slave. He spent five years as a shepherd before making a dramatic escape back across the Irish Sea to Cumbria. His faith had been strengthened by his ordeal and he made his way to France, where he trained as a priest, determined to return and convert his former tormentors.

His books shed light on the state of the church, and indeed the Solway area, in the period of the Roman withdrawal. He must have come from a fairly wealthy and sophisticated background as his father, Caporinus, was a deacon and his grandfather, Potius, had been a priest. Calporinus also had civic duties as a decurion, which meant that he would probably have been a man able to employ servants on his villa or estate. This

Exhibit depicting the visit of St Cuthbert, Tullie House Museum.

131

would suggest that the 'Bannaventa' mentioned as Patrick's birthplace would have had to have been a well-established place, with an organised Christian structure under the protection of a powerful chieftain or local leader. It would also have to have been on the western seaboard of Britain, within striking range of Irish pirates who would have needed a shrewd knowledge of the local tides and geography.

Interestingly, there are folk memories and legends that help to support the theory that Patrick was indeed Cumbrian. Tradition says that he preached in the Lake Country at Patterdale, where water issuing from a rock was used to baptise his converts and the little west Cumbrian town of Aspatria is said to commemorate him, its older name being 'Aspatrick'.

There is more fact than fiction in the story of St Kentigern, better known as St Mungo. He was one of the most important characters in the Church in Britain in the sixth and early seventh century. There are numerous references to him in ancient Welsh literature and in early mediaeval Arthurian chronicles and many of the oldest churches in north-west England are dedicated to him. He is famous for being the founder of Glasgow and re-Christianising large areas of Strathclyde and Rheged that had relapsed into the old pagan ways. At one point he was bishop of the whole of the kingdom of the North Britons and one of his bases was at Hoddom in Dumfriesshire, which was within the principality of Rheged. Recent excavations have revealed the foundations of a 16th-century church there. In around 553 he had to flee south to Wales and it wasn't until 573 that he was able to return. A crucial battle had

been won at Arthuret, where the pagan King Gwenddolau was defeated by the Christian King Rhydderch Hael of Strathclyde. He returned to Glasgow and died there on 13 January 613.

THE DEBATABLE LANDS AND THE SCOTS DYKE

Almost three and a half miles in length and built in 1552, the Scots Dyke was the first man-made frontier in Europe and formed part of the Border between the two countries. Much of it has now disappeared or is overgrown.

Drastic action had to be taken by the authorities when the law was in danger of completely breaking down and in the middle of the 15th century the Earl of Mar, who was regent at the time, decided to make an example of the more blatant outlaws who were openly wandering around the streets of Hawick. He surrounded the town and rounded up 53 Reivers. Six were hanged in Edinburgh, 18 were drowned, presumably in the river, because of a lack of trees or halters, and the remainder were either imprisoned or acquitted.

They got the message and the more desperate outlaws began to seek safety nearer the Border or even across it. Here they were in a sort of no man's land or demilitarised zone, where they could rob in whichever direction took their fancy. One of the largest of these 'debatable' lands was the area around Canonbie and Longtown, where there was no obvious boundary as the two countries had quarrelled over it so often. It

A long, curving line of trees marks the position of the Scots Dyke.

became an area of sanctuary, which the authorities preferred not to think about, and gathered about itself a motley collection of brigands, murderers and broken men. Various half-hearted efforts were made to clean up the place but the occupants were adept at playing one country off against the other, and they would switch their allegiance to any kingdom which offered them protection from the other.

Finally, Lord William Dacre, the warden of the English West March, lost his patience with Ill Will 'Sandy' Armstrong, one of the more notorious of his clan, who was complaining about the pressure that Lord Maxwell, the Scottish warden, was putting him under. The Grahams, who claimed to be English at the time, jumped on the bandwagon and threatened to 'become Scotchmen'.

Dacre refused to bow to blackmail and he set up a meeting with Maxwell to put and end to things once and for all. In 1551 a joint commission met to set up the building of a border or 'march dyke', and an agreement was finally reached on an earthwork running from the Esk just below its Liddle water to the Sark, which it was to follow until it reached the Solway.

Each end would be marked by a square stone bearing the arms of both countries.

GRETNA GREEN

Because it was the first village over the Border, Gretna became popular for runaway marriages. From 1754 the laws for marrying in England were different from those in Scotland.

Gretna Green Hall Hotel, reputedly once belonged to the Johnson family.

In England the couple had to be over 21, permission had to be given by both sets of parents and the ceremony had to take place in a church following the reading of wedding banns.

None of these conditions applied in Scotland, where marriage at 16 was allowed, and the village soon began to cash in on a very lucrative trade.

Most runaway marriages took place at the blacksmith's shop over the famous anvil, but couples of wealthier means went to Gretna Hall, an early 18th-century mansion once the home of the Johnstone family.

They had lived there since 1535 and their coat of arms can be seen over the doorway. Since 1793 it has been an elegant hotel, which still caters for hundreds of weddings a year. The hotel was very discreet and had a secret room, where runaway couples could hide from frantic fathers and Bow Street Runners.

Gretna Green Blacksmith's Shop, inside and out.

Gretna had an international reputation and in 1846 Miss Penelope Caroline Smythe, a wealthy heiress and reputed to be the most beautiful woman in Ireland, married an Italian Prince, Carlo Ferdinand Bourbon, brother to the King of Naples. The marriages were not always honourable affairs, however. Edward Gibbon Wakefield abducted 16-year-old Ellen Turner from her boarding school, claiming that her father owed him money and that marriage to him was the best way to cancel the debt. The marriage was eventually annulled by a special Act of Parliament and Wakefield was imprisoned. When released he emigrated to New Zealand to become its first Governor and later he was private secretary to the Governor-General of Canada!

Nearer to home the famous John Peel, the Cumbrian huntsman, brought his sweetheart here against her parents' wishes.

The Sark Bridge Toll House

This was the first dwelling in Scotland and it soon became apparent to its owners that it could intercept the couples heading for Gretna and offer them cheaper services. In 1830 it was run by Simon Beattie, who would enter into harmless conversation with the couples and lure them into accepting his rates. He succeeded, despite having an accent half Scottish and half Cumbrian that was difficult even for the locals to understand. He was quite a character, but he could make mistakes and overreach himself. There is the story of an old woman and her nephew returning from Carlisle Market, who took a long time explaining to him that they were not an eloping couple. Then there was a traveller who innocently asked a local woman for directions and Simon rushed out and tried to persuade them to get married. He was unsuccessful but still insisted that he could see no reason why they shouldn't have tied the knot.

A later owner, John Murray, was even more enterprising and reassured the couples that there was no need to go up to Gretna Hall as he could marry them just as well, for less money, and that the marriage would last just as long. He nearly went bankrupt, though, when he built a hotel a few yards away on the English side of the Border. It was just completed when Parliament moved the goalposts with the Brougham Act of 1856. This meant that before marrying legally in Scotland the couples had to have been in residence there for three weeks.

This law held until 1940, when, for a brief period, weddings in Scotland had to be held in a church or registry office. This was repealed in 1977 and once again Gretna became a favourite place for weddings. Today thousands still plight their troth there and the village is doing a roaring trade.

HAAF NETTING

The Haaf netters of both sides of the Solway are carrying on a tradition that stretches back to Viking times and, some people believe, even before that. 'Haaf' is the old Norse word for 'sea' or 'channel' and is a mobile frame, a bit like a five-a-side football goal with a central pole which the fishermen place upright, the net billowing out behind them. Both the beam and the net are handmade locally using traditional methods that have been passed down from generation to generation. The fishermen stand for hours, chest deep in the ebb or flow tides, adjusting their position when necessary and feeling the net for the slightest indication of a trapped salmon or sea trout.

It is a highly skilled and dangerous business. There are many tales of fishermen being swept away, especially by the ebb tides which race across the shallow flats out into the Irish Sea. The more adventurous will fish a section of a river channel that can suddenly change course as the tide meets it. This is known as a 'braid' and quite often a man will find himself drifting ashore clinging to his haaf in the wrong country. The unlucky ones will never be seen again. There is a story of haafnetter who had drunk a few pints too many while waiting for the tide and lost his footing. He drifted six miles upstream to Rockliffe, happily singing to himself and enjoying the ride, his waders having air filled pockets that kept him afloat! Another tale is of a small fishing boat whose crew heard strange noises in the dark next to their boat. They found a tramp with a bundle of clothes on his head swimmimg across to England.

A premium is placed, though, on local

Haaf Net Fishing.

knowledge of the river channels, tidal times and courses, and a safety measure includes moving from deep to shallow water when fishing with others in a line.

Today the few haafers that are left fish as a recreation. They have waterproof clothing, huge chest waders and are licensed to fish only from June to September, but in the 1800s men fished in ordinary clothes all year round to earn their living, and one way of fighting the cold was to bind the legs with coarse sacking.

Their prey is the Atlantic salmon and the sea trout. Giants of 30 pounds and over are now a rarity, mainly because the ancient feeding grounds off the Greenland coast have been discovered by commercial fishing fleets and numbers have been severely reduced in the past few years. The salmon leave their home rivers as tiny 'parr', only about six inches long, and they swim out into the Atlantic, feeding on krill and sea bed prawns. They grow rapidly and after a year some return to their home river as grilse of four to 10 pounds. Adult salmon spend two or three winters at sea and return as 10 or 20 pounders. Their ability to navigate over thousands of miles of ocean to their home river is, like bird migration, one of the great mysteries of nature. Sea trout are brown trout that move downstream into coastal waters to develop into adult fish. They are not as big as the salmon, but they can reach weights of up to eight pounds.

If the men are fishing in groups they sometimes use an ancient method for drawing lots called 'piling' or 'casting the mell'. They form a circle and each man kicks up a pile of sand and turns his back . The last man to arrive places a stone below one of the piles and they then turn around and kick over the piles until

it is found. The man who finds the stone chooses the best position. The most common method is to wade out to fish the ebb tide about four or five hours before the incoming or flood tide. The haaf is held facing the outgoing tide and any fish caught are carried in a bag on the fisherman's back. When the incoming tide is being fished, the line rotates up the shore as the tide rises, with the man in deepest water moving into the shallowest. On the English side the most commonly fished areas are between Bowness and Port Carlisle.

Other methods include 'Marsh' haafing, where the fisherman stays in one place on the bank and drops his net into the channel, and 'Shoaling', where fish are actually stalked in shallow water. This usually takes place two or three hours before the flood tide, again mainly between Bowness and Port Carlisle. A flicker of a dorsal fin or tail or ripples in the water alert the shoaler, who then races to the spot below the fish. He has to be careful not to let it sense his movement as he positions himself with a lowered net. He lines his beam up and runs with the bottom of it in the water to trap the fish. It is a highly skilful operation that demands good eyesight, speed and first class hand-eye coordination.

On the Scottish side, as well as haaf netting, there are poke and stake nets. Stake nets are basically channels of netting that trap incoming fish, and poke nets, now restricted to the parish of Annan, are iron stakes driven deep into the sand about four feet apart. A long net is fixed to the top and the bottom by iron rings that slide up and down the stake. One advantage of these methods is that the trapped salmon are seldom marked or injured and can fetch better prices in the market. In 2005 the ancient fishing rights on the Annan had been

Stake net fishing.

sold off and there was a question over the future of poke netting. Many of the stake net licences have also been bought out, mainly by The Atlantic Salmon Trust.

There were other forms of fishing on the Solway that have now vanished, such as 'Whammeling', 'Cobble netting' and 'Yair netting'. The first two involved a boat and nets and the latter was a small enclosure of nets built close to the shore in a curve. Paidle nets were designed to catch white fish or flounders, but they sometimes trapped salmon and the owners would face a hefty fine from the authorities if they were found out. In 1892 the fine was £8.15s or two months in gaol. Tempers would be short though because when times were hard this method of fishing was a basic source of food and income and there was often friction between the large landowners and the fishermen.

In addition to the estuary netting, there were also rich pickings to be had further out into the Irish Sea and in 1896 Annan had a fleet of 51 shrimp trawlers, 30 whammel boats, 13 herring boats and 24 smaller boats, but by the 1940s this fleet had shrunk to about twenty boats, mainly fishing for herring. With the advent of larger, better equipped vessels, the Annan fishermen had to move west to Kirkudbright and by 2004 all the boats had gone.

Sadly, it looks as if the haafnetters could face a similar plight. A hundred years ago there were over 400 of them on the Solway; today there are fewer than a 100. They feel that for a variety of reasons millionaire owners of private fishing and government departments are trying to close them down forever. In 2000 the number of licences were reduced and the season was shortened by almost four months, preventing fishing in May, the best month for the sea trout.

The haafnetters claim that there is no evidence that their traditional method of fishing has any effect at all on the number of fish entering the Rivers Eden, Esk or Annan. They point the finger at commercial salmon farming, the UDN disease in the period 1967 1972, and the discovery and over fishing of the feeding grounds off Greenland in the 1970s. The solutions could be in restocking, as has happened in the Tyne, now the finest salmon river in England, and restrictions on the hugely profitable commercial fishing fleets.

Note

In 1586 William Camden, the noted historian and map-maker, described how he observed Border Reivers spearing salmon in the Solway Firth. 'The district nourisheth a War-like kind of men, who have been infamous for Robberies and Depredations, for they dwell upon the Solway Firth, a fordable Arm of the Sea at Low Waters through which they made many times out-rodes into England for to fetch in Booties, and in which the inhabitants on both sides with pleasant pastime and delightful sight hunt Salmons of which there is an abundance.'

NB: This reference to the riders' great skill must have inspired Sir Walter Scott, who gives a vivid account of this in his novel, *Redgauntlet.*

THE JACOBITE REBELLIONS

Despite the union of the Crowns and Parliaments, there was still significant support for the Catholic Stuart monarchy in Scotland and parts of England. James Stuart, 'the Old Pretender' and son of James VII and II, was plotting in France and with his backing the Jacobites launched a rising in Scotland in 1715. It caused a stir but petered out in England at the Battle of Preston.

The rising found little support in Cumberland, but the city authorities took the precaution of locking up possible sympathisers such as Howard of Corby, Warwick of Warwick Hall and Curwen of Workington. There were moments of pure farce: two Companies of Chelsea Pensioners were sent north to deal with the 2,000 Jacobites. Having bypassed Carlisle they then passed within three miles of the Pensioners near Lancaster without noticing them. There

Jacobite Rebellion Exhibit — Carlisle Castle.

were prisoners taken but at the trials in the aftermath they were nearly all acquitted.

Not surprisingly, when Prince Charles Edward Stuart, the Old Pretender's son, raised his royal standard of blue, white and red silk at Glenfinnan on 23 July 1745, few people in Carlisle took any notice. The 'rash adventurer' was bound to fail, even though he had a legitimate claim to the United Crowns of England and Scotland. The Act of Union in 1707 had been grudgingly accepted by some but welcomed by most, as it ushered in peace and a growing prosperity. The Hanoverian royals, invited in to take the crown, were not yet fully anglicised, but they were accepted as a necessity and had a tolerance of the old Catholic religion that was welcomed by the recusant families still nervous of their status in a now Protestant country.

Their hesitance did not deter Charles one little bit. He would not let sleeping dogs lie, particularly as his grandfather's throne had been stolen, and, having been met by over 1,000 loyal Camerons and MacDonalds at

Bonnie Prince Charlie (original Tullie House Museum).

Portrait of Bonnie Prince Charlie in Carlisle – Tullie House Museum.

Glenfinnan, he was out to reclaim the kingship for the Stuarts. He was confident that he could revive the slumbering resentment of the old Jacobites, who had previously supported his father in 1715. By marching south he thought he could swell his Highland army with thousands of enthusiastic supporters who would join his cause. He was utterly wrong. Ignoring the advice of the majority of the Clan chiefs to return to France, he marched boldly on Edinburgh, and when his army of 6,000 Clansmen routed the army of General Cope at Prestonpans, alarm bells began to ring throughout the United Kingdom, especially in Carlisle and the Borders.

After the battle and in a glow of confidence he held elegant court at Holyrood House, charming all who met him. Thus began the legend of Bonnie Prince Charlie.

Opinion on the Borders was divided. While the Scottish Lowlands would be unlikely to show the same fervour as the Highlanders, there was lurking respect for the prince in northern England, particularly in Cumberland and Lancashire, which had shown Royalist sympathies during the Civil War. Carlisle had once been a Royalist city, and the man who was charged with its defence, Colonel Durand, found some of its citizens strangely unwilling to risk life and limb in its defence. The group that had most to gain from supporting the Hanoverian cause was the clergy. Dr John Waugh, chancellor of the diocese, prebendary of Carlisle and vicar of Stanwix, was the principal authority and chief supporter of Durand. The civil authority lay in the hands of the acting mayor, Thomas Pattinson. For some reason Waugh and Pattinson could not stand the sight of each other…

The castle, which was literally falling to bits, was garrisoned by 80 elderly veterans known as 'the invalids', a sort of 18th-century 'Dad's Army'. Reinforcing this meagre force were 500 infantry and 70 horse of the Cumberland and Westmoreland militia. Such was the state of Carlisle, the first line of defence in England in 1745.

Durand set about preparing for a two-month siege; he had cannon mounted on the walls, ammunition collected, sandbags made, all ladders in the outlying areas collected, the water supply checked, all shrubbery near the walls cut down and the city checked for spies. Finally, he posted two clergymen on the cathedral tower as lookouts.

By now the Highlanders were advancing on the city in two columns through the Borders, one via Peebles and Moffat and the other via Kelso and Lauder. The army was met with sullen indifference by the Lowlanders, with one or two individual exceptions who would later suffer the consequences, and when one of the baggage wagons was left behind at Ecclefechan, because of the poor state of the road, a party of men from Dumfries, regaining their Reiver instincts, attacked and looted it.

The two columns met on the morning of 9 November and forded the Eden at Rockliffe, five miles north of Carlisle. A local countryman was used to take a message to the city authorities to provide quarters for 13,000 foot and 5,000 horse. This was plainly a bluff intended to shock the inhabitants into submission – the Highland army would have been around 6,000 men at most – and when an advance party appeared on Stanwix Bank later that afternoon,

Colonel Durand fired cannonballs at them and they vanished.

Seventy miles away, eastwards through the Tyne gap, an English army under General Wade was expected to come to the city's relief, but it was now approaching winter and the roads proved impassable. The citizens realised they were on their own and Charles sent a second message warning of the dire consequences of showing resistance. The clergy and 'several notabilities' bravely guarded the walls that night, but when the local militia deserted their posts Colonel Durand had no option but to surrender the city. On Monday 18 November Charles made his entry into Carlisle seated on a white charger and preceded by not less than 111.

By now there were three armies gathering in England to deal with him, but he marched south to Derby and was poised to take the capital. This was the prince's finest hour, but his advisers wanted to go no further. In London there was open panic and it is said that if the Jacobites had known of the terror that their advance had caused, they would not have stopped. Charles strongly opposed the retreat, but he was back in Carlisle on 19 December with his now demoralised clansmen strung out behind him all the way back to Penrith.

Close on his heels was the Duke of Cumberland, the third son of George II. Although still a young man, he was already an experienced campaigner and he had a brief to stamp out the Jacobites once and for all. The prince left a garrison of 400 men behind him to defend the city as he headed north to Edinburgh and what he thought would be safety. His plans to rendezvous with a French invading force and return to Carlisle were pure fantasy and these men were virtually agreeing to commit suicide.

Cumberland dismissed the castle contemptuously as 'an old hen coop', fired a few cannonballs at it and took the surrender. He soon had the doomed garrison cooped up as prisoners in appalling conditions in the castle dungeons. The rest of the story is well known. Charles was tracked all the way to Culloden, where his Highlanders were cut to pieces by Cumberland on 16 April 1746. Cumberland was given the task of pacifying the Highlands, which he accomplished with an unrelenting cruelty, debauchery and barbarism. In England a flower was named after him in his honour, a 'Sweet William'. In Scotland it was called a 'Stinking Billy', and he also became known as 'the Butcher'.

To celebrate the victory a new anthem, composed by Handel and dedicated to George II, was sung in London and was called *God Save our Gracious King*. There was little that could save the prisoners in Carlisle Castle, however. Thirty-one of the 382 of them were condemned to death and most of the rest were transported for life to the American colonies. The penalty for treason at that time was still the horrific hanging, drawing and quartering. This grisly event took place on Harraby Hill, a mile south of the city, where a modern hotel now stands. It was reported that each one of the men met their deaths bravely and one young prisoner called Cappock was said to have cheered up his companions with the reassurance that in the next world they wouldn't be tried by a Cumberland jury…

Apart from a new national anthem, another song has come down to us from those times. *Loch Lomond* is said to have originated from one of the prisoners in the castle. By taking the 'low road' (death), he would be home in Scotland 'afore ye'.

ROMAN SOLWAY

A popular misconception is that Hadrian's Wall was the limit of the Empire and that everything north of it was a barbarian wasteland. In Celtic Britain, though, the Solway was not a frontier but probably a well-populated and civilised area, which suddenly had to deal with foreign invaders.

There are two museum pieces from different sides of the Solway that suggest that there was a flourishing, highly-developed, artistic, though warlike, culture that was far from barbaric. The first is the jewelled Embleton sword from Cumbria, now in the British Museum, and the other is a fabulous horse's mask from Kirkudbrightshire. This once sat proudly in Sir Walter Scott's study and is now in the National Museum of Scotland. They are both examples of superb craftsmanship possibly originating from the Novantae and Brigantes tribes who populated the area that the Romans were invading.

General Julius Agricola began the first serious attempt at subduing what the Romans called the Caledonians or North Britons in AD79. The Romans had already been met with several great risings, Boudicca's in the south being just one of them. One of the kings of the North, Venuitius, fortified Stanwick near Scotch Corner, but he was defeated and he fled into the Solway area. Agricola marched north and

established a base in Carlisle from which to try to conquer Scotland, building a turf and wood fort on the exact spot where the cathedral stands today.

Excavations in Annandale suggest that there had been earlier, unsuccessful attempts to penetrate the land, with evidence of forts and marching camps in the Dumfries and Galloway valleys and hilltops. Having secured his base, Agricola marched further north, but found it increasingly difficult to manoeuvre his troops in the mountains and forests of the Highlands and, after a victory at the battle of Mons Graupius in AD83, he and his 10,000-strong army were recalled to Rome by the Emperor.

Forty years later the Emperor Hadrian was forced to abandon the Scottish conquests and consolidate his frontier by building a wall across the narrow Tyne–Solway isthmus. It became the best-known frontier in the entire Roman empire and the parts that still stand today are an astonishing reminder of its genius and will-power. It took six years to build and the work was carried out by legionaries complemented by ranks of skilled craftsmen such as surveyors, architects, carpenters and engineers.

Carlisle was then known as Luguvalium,

The Site of Stanwix Roman cavalry fort just above the banks of the River Eden.

The Roma Wall ended on the Solway near Bowness.

Statue of Fortuna, the Goddess of fate and good luck.

Woman with fan and child.

and it was completely replanned as a civilian settlement with the military garrison being transferred to Stanwix on the north side of the River Eden. This was the largest camp on the entire wall and housed the Alia Petriana, an elite cavalry division which could race to trouble spots in a matter of minutes along the Stanegate – a Roman road running parallel to the wall.

There are few traces of the wall left in the Solway area, as many of the stones have been liberated by farmers and settlers over the years to build houses and barns, but at certain sections the vallum or ditch can clearly be seen. The wall ended at Bowness on Solway, the last fordable point to Scotland, and for 25 miles to the south-west a series of forts was built to deal with any naval threat from Ireland or southern Scotland.

For about 250 years the citizens of Luguvalium enjoyed peace and prosperity, relishing a high standard of living that would not reappear until our own 20th century. The layout of the city would probably be recognisable to one of them even today. The Market Cross stands on the site of the Forum and the roads that radiate out from the Town Hall were built on top of Roman foundations. The final curtain fell in AD410 when pressure on the eastern frontier and slave rebellions at home forced the emperor to withdraw his legions back to Rome.

SOLWAY SMUGGLING

There are colourful tales of quick-witted locals outwitting the local custom men and quaffing their tax-free whisky around a roaring winter's fire, but the reality was far

The English Solway — looking towards Cardurnock at dusk.

less romantic. The low-level cheating by ordinary citizens, sometimes given a nod and a wink by colluding excise men themselves, gradually gave way to some ruthless sharp practice from organised gangs as the government in the 18th century imposed harsh laws on all contraband. Tensions were further increased when the death penalty for smuggling was introduced. Now anyone informing on the smuggling gangs would be in severe danger…

It had all begun to get serious in the 13th century when Edward I, who crops up regularly in this book, started to raise money for his invasion of Wales by placing a tax on wool leaving the country. This was a heavy blow to the multitude of sheep farmers, who now had to pay a 40 percent duty on each bag of wool they produced.

Whether or not the holy monks of Holme Cultram Abbey, who kept herds of over 6,000 sheep, dabbled in dodgy trade is not certain, but over the next few hundred years

smuggling was virtually a second occupation for hard-pressed communities on both sides of the Solway. An additional incentive was that the nearby Isle of Man was a tax-free area. During the 1700s there was continual 'business' between the island and the coastlines of Cumbria and southern Scotland. Quite often overstretched customs men would be faced with fleets of 10 or more small ships, which would saturate the coasts with their goods. These officers would also face the problem of finding witnesses who would testify in court against the smugglers. The money being made was welcomed by all members of the community, even by local officials and Members of Parliament, and there were consistent reports of corruption at all levels of society on both sides of the Border. Bringing a conviction was almost impossible, and anyway, there was a fair degree of sympathy from on high. Sir Walter Scott in *The Heart of Midlothian* referred to the repressive laws as 'an unjust aggression on

Boats on the mud flats of the Scottish Solway near Old Graitney.

'Dubs' of turf on the English Solway near Bowness.

their (smugglers) ancient liberties'.

The smugglers took risks. In 1750 John Frost from the Back of the Hill near Annan was found guilty of 'having in his possession quantities of spirits for which he could not account'. The sheriff sentenced him to jail for three months but first 'to be whipped publicly through the streets of Dumfries. To be tied to a cart to receive 30 lashes at the foot of the Bridge Vennel, 30 at the Fish Cross and 30 at the Kirkgate Port and thereafter remanded to prison until the 28 August upon which day to undergo the same punishment again, then to be banished from the County for life'.

Sometimes you could hardly blame them. Scottish farmers, who would be living on a weekly wage of six shillings a week, would risk their necks to get Cumberland coal back across the channels for a shilling a load. In Scotland it would have cost them five times that.

One notable excise man was Robbie Burns, who needed extra money to supplement his income from his farming at Ellisland. Based in Dumfries, his territory covered 10 parishes and he would often have to travel 200 miles a week on horseback to oversee things. In 1791 he was paid an annual salary of £50 a year and he had to provide his own horse.

He had an understanding eye, though. A local mother called Jean Dean was suspected of smuggling after an annual fair. She was tipped off that Burns would be inspecting her house and she vanished, leaving a servant and a small girl in charge. The servant protested that there were no spirits in the house but the little girl innocently announced that that was not true and that the cellar was full of bottles of ale. Burns explained that he and his men were in a hurry and that they would return later, by which time the bottles had, of course, disappeared.

Another story has him watching over a stranded lugger on the Dumfries sands. He was posted to keep watch and he whiled away the hours by composing a rhyme, which suggested that his heart wasn't really in it.

'Well mak' our mautan' bre our drink,
We'll dance and sing, and rejoice man
An' mony thanks to the muckle blacked'ill
That danced awa wi' the Exciseman.'

When the smuggler's ship was broken up he bought its four brass cannon and sent them south as a token of sympathy with the French Revolutionaries. The authorities were not amused and they were impounded at Dover.

Much effort was put into secreting whisky across the Border where it would fetch a handsome price. In 1820 Parliament decided to step in and an Act was passed prohibiting the carrying of whisky into England by land. It also provided that anyone carrying in or selling such spirits should forfeit 40 shillings for every gallon or incur a penalty of £100.

Naturally, this didn't deter the locals and there were frequent reports of skirmishes and marshy chases between the officials and the authorities, particularly around the fords on the Sark, Eden and Esk estuaries.

The excisemen had to be constantly on their toes to catch people out. Whisky would be hidden in knapsacks, cheese boxes, trunks, canteens, milk cans and even haaf nets. Some of these containers were adapted to fit the bodies of women to give them what was euphemistically called 'a certain appearance'. One of them held four gallons of whisky... One likely lad was trying to bypass Rockliffe on an old road to Carlisle when he was challenged. He was carrying spirits in pig bladders and he swiftly tied them to his dog, pushed it in the river and somehow made him swim to the other bank where he was hauled out by an accomplice.

Some houses had secret entries below the fireplace – with a good fire burning in the grate when the excisemen appeared – and there was even a flat gravestone beside Annan town hall which contained no body but a wood-lined grave for the safe storage of goods. Annan was also home to a famous smuggler called Morice Bell, who was arrested near Gretna one evening when several kegs were found at the bottom of his light cart. He was arrested, but on the way to Annan he was able to quietly remove one keg at a time, memorising the places on the roadside where each one was hidden.

This lighter side of the 'trade' was captured in Kipling's famous poem, where the advice is to turn a blind eye and 'watch the wall my darling as the gentlemen go by'. But as the profits increased there were very few gentlemen about and the excisemen ran a real risk of being murdered. These smugglers were not loveable scoundrels but sophisticated criminals and anyone who got in their way would find themselves in deep trouble. There were frequent complaints, by the customs collector in Carlisle, for example, that his men were intimidated by the sheer scale of the smuggling and also the threatening nature of the gangs they tried to stop.

The gangs were perfecting their methods all the time. Ships would sail at night with black sails and landing points on the coast would be carefully chosen to allow swift dispersal under cover of darkness. Lookouts on shore would watch out for the excisemen and batmen would patrol the area and

The Scottish side of the Solway viaduct remains – Annan.

threaten any unwanted persons. Sometimes the goods were dropped about a quarter of a mile offshore on the seaward side of boats, so that they could not be seen from the land. These would be weighted down and marked with what looked like seagulls, but were in fact pig bladders covered in feathers. From a distance they looked like the real thing. At low tide later that night the goods would be recovered.

Inevitably the Government cracked down and encouraged people to inform with promises of rewards and smuggling began to decline. Undoubtedly its heyday has passed but maybe its legacy lingers on. There were rumours that during World War Two the Cumbrian farmers, who were aware of rationing laws, always seemed to look in robust health and had more money than usual to spend…

SOLWAY VIADUCT

Spanning the shortest crossing point of the Firth between Bowness on Solway and Annan, the railway viaduct was opened in 1869. It shortened the route for Lancashire iron ore to be taken to the Lanarkshire

steelworks in Scotland. The engineer was Sir James Brunlees and he was proud of constructing, across the shifting Solway sands, what was then the longest bridge in Britain. It had a short life, though, as nature began to pay it attention. The Tay Bridge disaster was still a hideous memory and the viaduct was severely damaged in 1875 when ice got into the hollow iron pillars and cracked them. Six years later, in 1881, during what became known as 'the great freeze', the upper reaches of the Esk and Eden froze over and when they thawed on 29 January massive ice blocks began to sweep down to the open sea. Carried along by an ebb current, they were moving at 10 to 15 miles an hour.

On a cabin in the middle of the structure sat four terrified watchmen. They later described the sound of the ice floes hitting the pillars as being like artillery fire. The viaduct was shuddering and they ran for their

The English remains of the Solway viaduct seen from Bowness.

Solway Viaduct remain at Herdhill Scar near Bowness.

lives. Next morning it was falling to pieces and sparks were to be seen as steel fell against steel. There were two gaps of 50 and 300 yards. Extensive repairs were carried out and it was regularly used again until 1914. From 1914 to 1920 no passenger trains were carried, though especially light trains continued to carry iron ore to Clydeside.

By 1921 the bridge was considered unsafe and closed to traffic. Not all traffic…thirsty Scotsmen would defy the Sabbath by walking across to Bowness for a welcome pint or two of Sassenach beer, despite the chance of being fined if caught. Final demolition work began in March 1935, but sadly three young men working in a boat on the side of one of the pillars were swept away by a treacherous current. The notorious combination of a strong south-west wind and a flood tide roared up the Solway. Their boat crashed into a set of poke nets on the Scottish shore and was overturned.

The photograph shows the remains of the steel pillars on the end of the sandstone embankment. From here it is still possible to walk across to another country at low tide, but only with an experienced guide.

THE SOLWAY WATHS

The waths were the ancient crossing places where local knowledge of tides and quicksands could ensure a reasonably safe crossing. For centuries kings, smugglers, Reiver bands and invading armies from north and south would dash across the sands before the next tide began to sweep in. It was a risky business, though, even with guides; a half-hour's miscalculation can cost you your life. The tides can fill the horizon in a matter of minutes and if the rivers are in spate and the wind is swirling in from the south and west, the water charges in as a wave that can reach two to three feet high. Even on the marshes, the little muddy creeks can fill alarmingly quickly, cutting off that safe link to higher ground. It is sometimes the sound of the tide that is first.

Timing is crucial. When retreating with an army or rustled cattle it was essential to know exactly when and where to cross. A determined rearguard could delay its escape until the last minute by plunging into the widening channels, knowing that pursuit would be suicidal. It did not always work, however. In the chaos of battle and retreat

almost 2,000 Scots were drowned in the Eden estuary in February 1216 near the Peat Wath. King John had invaded Scotland and in retaliation King Alexander II made a destructive counter raid into Cumberland. Against his instructions a band of his followers pillaged Holme Cultram Abbey and had to cross the Eden on their way back to Scotland. They miscalculated…

Sometimes these armies had little choice, as passing near fortified Carlisle and chancing a swollen River Eden was more risky than a longer estuary detour and crossing.

It is still possible to identify the main crossings or waths from historical evidence. The three most frequently used were the Sulwath, the Peatwath and the Bowness or Annanwath. Upstream towards Carlisle there were other minor ones at Cargo and Rockliffe.

Finding out precisely where these waths were is not easy, however, since the Rockliffe

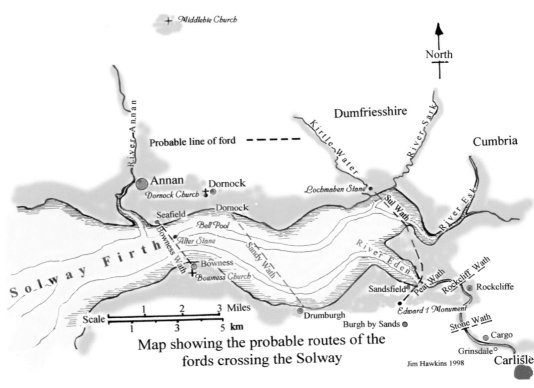

Map by kind permission of Jim Hawkins of Annan.

Map showing the probable routes of the fords crossing the Solway

Jim Hawkins 1998

The Solway Firth is a treacherous trap of mud flats and quicksand for the unwary.

marsh has expanded by about three miles seaward since 1400. In addition the channels of the four rivers, the Esk, Eden, Sark and Kirtle, which flow into the eastern end of the estuary, are constantly changing. The north to south crossing of the Sulwath would most likely have started near the Lochmabenstone near Gretna on the Scottish side and ended near Rockliffe on the English side. This was a frequently used one and Sulwath, meaning 'muddy ford', probably changed into 'Solway' over the years.

The Sandywath or Dornockwath was found a few miles west, starting on Burgh marsh. This was a longer crossing but had the advantage of being wide, open and relatively shallow, giving plenty of time for manoeuvre and retreat if necessary.

The shortest wath was between Annan and Bowness, and this was used frequently in the Scottish wars of independence by William Wallace and King Edward I.

Edward knew the Solway well. He died near the Peatwath in 1307 on his way to yet another invasion of Scotland, and coins from his reign have been found near his monument on Burgh marsh, where his vast army was preparing to cross. Other crossings are the Stonywath, a couple of miles upstream on the Eden, Grinsdale and Cargo waths (used by Prince Charles Stuart and the Highland army in 1745) and the Etterby wath opposite Carlisle Castle. This latter one was thought to have been used by the ancient

Crossing The Waths can be highly dangerous and should only be attempted in the company of a skilful and experienced guide.

British. A track starting near Shap Fell reaches the river here and it was on this spot that the Roman wall spanned the river.

In later years cattle drovers delivering stock to the London markets used these fords, particularly the Annan–Bowness one as it was a considerable short cut to the south, and the last recorded one was in 1863. Thereafter it became much cheaper to transport the animals by train and the newly-built viaduct in 1869 made crossing here very difficult.

It should be pointed out here that using these routes is extremely hazardous and should never be attempted without a guide. It could also be worth mentioning that the author and his cousins, when small children, used to cross to Scotland from Bowness when on holiday and they lived to tell the tale…

Location of Bowness Wath.

Opposite: The Bowness Wath crosses from Seafield to Bowness.

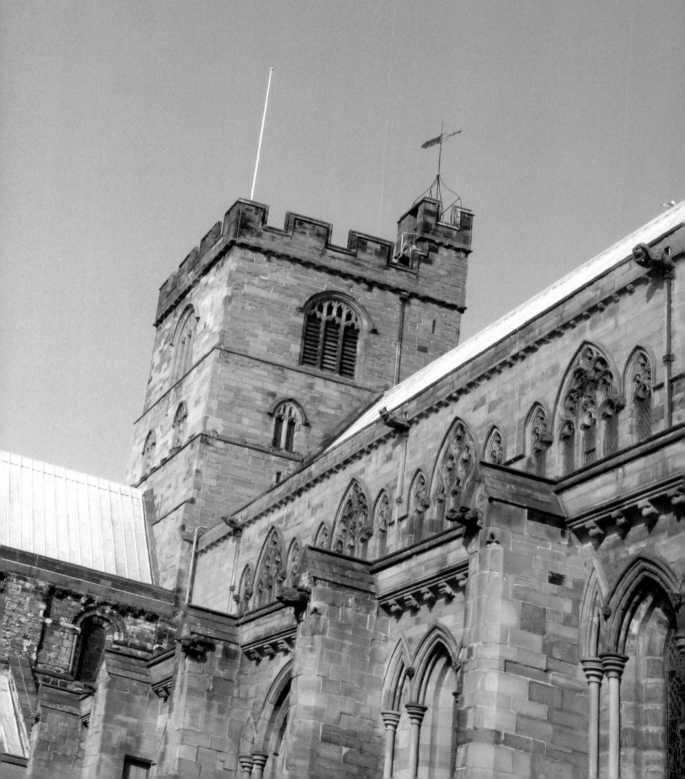

Carlisle

Previous page: Carlisle Cathedral was founded in 1133.

Ram-horn god sculpture — Tullie House Museum.

Roman altars — Tullie House Museum.

CARLISLE — GENERAL

Ram-horned god
This Celtic god is one of the...

An ancient British ford crosses the River Eden a few hundred yards downstream of the main bridge. It is a clue that Carlisle had a significance as a pivotal point in the area well before the Romans. There is little trace of earlier settlements but it is possible that it was a defensive site of a fierce, independent warlike tribe called the Brigantes, who held and defended the land against the invaders. The Celtic prefix 'caer' (a place of strength), and 'Lywell', a British prince, was its first name and the Romans called it Lugavallium – a town or fort on the Roman wall dedicated to the god of light, Lug. They recognised its superb defensive possibilities, building a fort on a sloping mound protected by three rivers. In time this would develop into a formidable Norman castle. In AD120 Hadrian built his famous wall, stretching across the narrow isthmus between the Solway and the Tyne, and Carlisle was its principal bulwark.

The Romans stayed for nearly four centuries and then a dark fog descends with few accurate records of who came next. It is known, however, that after the Romans withdrew it remained a powerful and independent centre of British power and there are persistent legends that a dynamic Christian leader organised a brilliant guerilla campaign against the pagan Saxons encroaching from the east and the Picts from the north. Could this have been '*Rex quondam Rex futuris*', Arthur, the

once and future king? Some Arthurian scholars claim that they are closing in on the Border area as his realm and that many of his 12 battles were fought in this region. They even claim that Carlisle could have been one of his 'Camelots'. Whatever the truth, there is no doubt that over the next 1,200 years the city became the fighting capital of the Borders and a vital pawn in the power struggle between England and Scotland.

In the seventh century it was possibly the capital city of the kingdom of Rheged and had Coel Hen, or 'Old King Cole', as one of its early regents. Rheged was then taken over by the Saxon King Egfrith, who had been converted to Christianity, and St Cuthbert was a visitor to the city in 686. The Venerable Bede wrote that:

'The next day when the citizens were leading him to see the walls of the town and the remarkable fountain, formerly built by the Romans, suddenly, as he was resting on his staff, he was disturbed in spirit.'

The fact that he was being shown round by Queen Earmenburga and his appreciation of the magnificence of the Roman ruins indicates that, at that time, Carlisle was a place of some

*St Cuthbert's visit
to Carlisle exhibit
— Tullie House.*

importance. What he was being disturbed by must remain a mystery, though.

The records are scanty but it is known that Halfdan the Dane sacked Carlisle towards the end of the ninth century, killing every man, woman and child in the city and burning every building to the ground. Charred remains of this calamity can sometimes be found in the various archaeological digs of recent years. Then, in 945, it came under the control of Malcolm, King of Scotland, and remained under his rule until about 1070.

Enter the Normans: William the Red, the son of William I, was returning from Alnwick to Carlisle having concluded a peace treaty with the King of Scotland and he 'observed the pleasantries of its situation and resolved to raise it from its ruins'. He began work on the castle, established a priory and built the massive city walls. His work was eventually completed by Henry I, who awarded the church its cathedral status. The Scots understandably still looked to Cumbria as being a part of their territory and in 1136 King David took the city by storm and held the Great Council of Scottish Kings in the city. He died there in 1153 and during the latter years of his reign Carlisle was effectively the capital city of Scotland.

It was becoming a political tennis ball, however: Henry II of England took the city

back, but his successor King John lost control of it to King Alexander II in 1216. Finally, the city became permanently English under Henry III.

Edward I, or 'Longshanks' as he was known, recognised Carlisle's potential as a border fortress and under him it became a formidable military centre. He held his Parliament here with all the trappings of medieval pageantry and he used the city as his base of operations in the Scottish wars. It was at this point that peace became a mere memory and for the next 400 years there was almost continual war between the two countries, with Carlisle bearing the brunt of the conflict.

In March 1296 a Scottish army of 40,000 under the Earl of Buchan besieged the city and the citizens put up a fierce resistance. An enemy spy escaped from his prison and set fire to the city. While the menfolk were fighting the blaze, the women were hurling stones and throwing boiling oil on the Scots. One unfortunate Scottish leader, while setting fire to one of the city gates, was fished up in the air with a large hook and then killed by the defenders' lances. This so discouraged the besiegers that they immediately withdrew.

King Edward's campaigns of 1298 and 1300 brought a fragile peace, but Wallace's execution and Robert the Bruce's coronation in Scotland in 1306 signalled trouble. The old warrior died on Burgh Marsh in 1307, breathing defiance at his enemy until the last. In 1315 Bruce besieged the city a year after his sensational victory at Bannockburn and again in 1332.

Not surprisingly, Carlisle was not a rich and prosperous place. It had to be constantly on guard, there was little time for commerce and its outlying areas, particularly to the north, became very dangerous places indeed. During

Seige gun –
Carlisle citadel.

Carlisle Market Hall.

Carlisle Market Hall clock.

the reign of Henry VIII the Border was comparatively quiet, but his preoccupation with his wars in France meant that he was always looking nervously north to see what its allies, the Scots, were up to. In 1542 a large Scottish army was defeated by a smaller English one at the battle of Solway Moss, only a few miles north of the city.

During Queen Elizabeth I's reign, in 1568, the castle 'held' another royal visitor, the doomed Mary Queen of Scots, on her way south to her inevitable execution a few years later at Fotheringay Castle.

During the Civil Wars the city was firmly royalist and when York surrendered to Cromwell's Roundheads in 1644, the commander of the king's forces on the north, Sir Thomas Glemham, escaped to Carlisle. Once again the city was under siege, this time from a Scottish general, Sir David Leslie. The citizens held out for 10 months and were reduced to eating rats and dogs, but they negotiated an honourable surrender. When an emissary was allowed to enter to discuss terms they got him so drunk on ale that he could hardly stand. When he returned he was convinced that the city still had plentiful supplies and they secured more favourable terms.

Carlisle was bypassed by the Jacobites in the first rebellion in 1715 but in 1745 Prince Charles Edward Stuart marched in with his Highland army and King James III was proclaimed from Carlisle Cross. On his return a few months later he was in full retreat and once more the city was in Government hands. His campaign marked the final goodnight to the endless jockeying for control and calmer times were ahead.

The city did not shed its violent past immediately, however; in 1813 a 15-year-old boy was publicly whipped and imprisoned for a month for stealing a handkerchief, there was still bull baiting on the sands until 1824 and a duel was fought with pistols at nearby Kingmoor in 1827.

By the beginning of the 19th century, however, the judiciary was becoming more enlightened. The textile trade was firmly established and the city began to grow and prosper. In 1876 the Citadel station was the terminus of seven railway companies and brewing, construction, metal box making and even biscuit manufacturing was providing steady employment for a growing population. The Victorian period saw Carlisle emerging as a confident, energetic city.

Time lends it a romantic glow: King Arthur, Merlin, St Cuthbert, Mary Queen of Scots and

Part of The Guildhall in Carlisle is now an Italian Ristorante.

Bonnie Prince Charlie are a glamorous parade, but to the average citizen living in pre-20th century times, it must have been anything but.

Carlisle Guildhall

In the Middle Ages tradesmen began to protect themselves by forming special associations or 'Guilds'. Carlisle had eight: butchers, merchants, shoemakers, skinners, tanners, smiths, tailors and weavers. They would meet in the Guildhall, each in their own room. The building is the only mediaeval house left standing in the city. It was originally called Redness Hall after a merchant called Richard de Redness, who owned it in the days of Richard II (1377–1399).

The meetings were jolly and colourful affairs, with 'spiced cakes, cake-breed and Sondry wines' helping the proceedings to go with a swing. The rooms would be decorated with expensive cloths and tapestries as well as the banners of the individual guilds. One of the highlights of the year was Ascension Day or Holy Thursday, when the whole city was roused by the sound of fifes and drums and a procession of the great and the not so great would follow the bands and banners up to Kingmoor for a day of eating, drinking and horse racing.

Tullie House

This elegant old house, built around 1689 and now part of an award-winning museum, belonged to the Tullies. They were a wealthy Carlisle family descended from a German miner, whom Queen Elizabeth I brought over to work the gold and silver mines near Keswick. It was bought by public subscription and given to the city Corporation in 1892.

Tullie House Museum, Carlisle.

Carlisle Cross

This was the centre of the old Roman city and the present cross, standing opposite the Town Hall, was erected in 1682. It was from here that Prince Charles Edward Stuart was proclaimed king of England and Scotland in 1745. Earlier, the birth of his father in 1688 had been greeted with delight by Irish officers who lit a great bonfire next to the castle. They certainly knew how to celebrate...

'They drank wine there till, with that and the transport of the news, they were exceedingly distracted, throwing their hats into the fire at one health, their coats the next, their waistcoats at the third, and so on to their shoes, and some of them ran about naked like madmen.'

For the past 600 years, Carlisle Great Fair has been proclaimed at eight o' clock in the morning on 26 August from this very spot, heralding a colourful week of stalls, side shows, period dressing-up and sports events.

Carlisle and the Railways

In its heyday in the early part of the 20th century, Carlisle was second only to London as a railway terminus. There were seven companies operating through it: the North British; the Caledonian; the Glasgow and South Western; the London and North Western; the Maryport and Carlisle; the North Eastern and the Midland. It was a hugely important communications centre and all of these companies had their own separate goods yards and engine sheds.

The first to open was the Carlisle to Newcastle line in 1838, and it was soon realised that a large station would have to be built to accommodate all the increase in traffic that was to follow. In 1847 Sir William Tite, who had earlier designed the Bank of England and the Royal Exchange, used a Tudor-Gothic style to build the imposing Citadel Station.

In those early days third-class travel was an

Carlisle "Railway City" exhibit, Tullie House Museum.

becalmed condition belies its violent and dramatic story. Sometimes in Scottish hands, mostly in English, it has been a political tennis ball throughout its 1,000 years as a pivotal defensive site on England's northern frontier.

It was the Romans who first recognised that the rising mound flanked by three rivers had superb defensive potential, but their wooden fort is long since gone and it wasn't until 1092 that King William (Rufus) II, exasperated by Scottish raids, rebuilt it. Thirty years later his brother, Henry I, started work on the city walls and built the massive red sandstone keep.

King David I claimed the castle for Scotland in 1157, completed most of the work and later, once more in English hands, Henry II strengthened it even further.

In the next 100 years the castle saw bitter and bloody fighting. William the Lion of Scotland besieged it twice and then Alexander II raised the Scottish standard on its ramparts. After he withdrew the formidable Edward I (Longshanks) made Carlisle his base for his invasion of Scotland. His presence was partly in response to the terrifying raids of William (Braveheart) Wallace, who had been

adventure; the carriages were simply open trucks with wooden seats and 'one writer suggested that a netting should be hooked under each carriage just under the footboard to prevent passengers being thrown under the wheels…'

Carlisle Castle

In 1745 the Duke of Cumberland (known to the Scots as 'the Butcher of Culloden') dismissed the castle as 'an old hen coop', but to the preceding generations it was anything but. It was the most formidable fortress on the Borders and even today its massive red sandstone walls dominate the northern skyline of the city.

History hovers over the place. Its present

The Keep – Carlisle Castle.

harrying the Borders and Cumberland before heading back north.

After Wallace was executed in 1305, Robert the Bruce seized the throne of Scotland. Edward hurried back, had royal apartments installed and in 1306, when Parliament met in Carlisle, the castle became the seat of government. Edward died at nearby Burgh-by-Sands in July 1307, and after the disastrous Battle of Bannockburn, 'the Bruce' once more swept south with Carlisle bearing the brunt of his attacks in 1315. According to the records, that particular summer was appallingly wet and Robert's huge assault tower collapsed in the mud. Attempts at mining the walls were a farce because of the flooding and his army trudged home in disgust.

It was besieged again in 1461 during the Wars of the Roses, when the House of Lancaster made an unusual alliance with 'hungrie Scottis' against the House of York and then there was a period of peace until the reign of Henry VIII. Muttering Catholics, upset at the separation from Rome, had organised a northern rebellion (the Pilgrimage of Grace). Henry was very conscious of the growing anti-Protestant alliance between France, Scotland and Spain and decided it was time to reinforce and fortify the castle against any possible trouble on his northern border.

A famous 'visitor' to the castle in May 1568 was Mary Queen of Scots, who was really a prisoner of her cousin, Queen Elizabeth I. She stayed for the months of June and July, amusing herself as best she could with walks along the ramparts and watching her retinue play football on the riverbanks below the castle. She then continued her doomed journey south...

Opposite: The Gatehouse — Carlisle Castle..

The Battery, Carlisle Castle.

If the castle held a queen a prisoner it couldn't hold one of the notorious Reivers, Kinmont Willie Armstrong. He had been captured during a truce at Kershopfoot by the vengeful Musgrave and Salkeld families in 1596 and imprisoned in the castle. Even though he was a well-known thief, this was a flagrant breach of trust and Sir Walter Scott of Buccleuch set out to rescue him. On a dark stormy night he forded the swollen Esk and Eden rivers with 80 men and took the castle guards completely by surprise. By morning the entire party was safely back in Scotland with a jubilant Kinmont Willie.

Carlisle backed the Stuarts in the 1600s and a Scottish army dug in for an eight-month siege in October 1644. Reduced to eating rats and hearing of King Charles's defeat at Naseby, the Cavaliers left the city and the Scots army marched in. They repaired the city walls with stone taken from the cathedral, reinforced the castle and were in turn driven out by a Parliamentarian force.

The 15th century prisoners' carvings — Carlisle Castle.

In November 1745 Prince Charles Edward Stuart (Bonnie Prince Charlie), preceded by his 'hundred pipers an all', appeared dramatically on Stanwix Bank to the north of the city and demanded its surrender. He was invading England to claim what he thought was his rightful throne. Returning to Scotland in December, after the loss of nerve at Derby, he garrisoned the castle with a small rearguard. His royal cousin the Duke of Cumberland accepted its surrender after a few cannonballs had smashed into the castle walls.

Which brings us back to the Jacobite prisoners… They had little chance of mercy and one brave Highlander told the court that he hoped for better justice in the next life when he would not be facing a 'Cumbrian jury'. Eleven men suffered the ultimate penalty and were led out of the castle on hurdles to Harraby Hill. Apparently some of the citizens who had come to watch were so disgusted by the executions that they vowed never to attend such a barbaric ceremony again. It is also said that the famous song *Loch Lomond* was composed by a Highland prisoner in the castle, who, by taking the low road home (death), would be in Scotland before his friends who would take the high road.

The macabre 'licking stone' Carlisle Castle dungeons.

The dungeons, the Keep, Carlisle Castle.

Ripples from the French Revolution reached Carlisle in 1792 and it began to remember its radical past. There were corn riots, anti-slavery gatherings and wild rumours of discontent. The Government responded by flooding the castle with loyal troops, and building new barracks and an armoury. By 1848 the crisis was over but the army had come to stay.

It has been the training area of the Border Regiment since 1881 and in 1959, although the main body of soldiers moved on, it had become the regimental headquarters with its own museum in the inner castle.

If you half close your eyes and try to ignore the hum of 20th-century traffic just outside its walls, it is still possible to imagine the Redcoats, Highlanders, siege engines and tragic queens that have made up its extraordinary story.

The warden's apartments, built in 1378, were a later addition to the castle and were meant to provide comfortable accommodation for the wardens of the marches. They had a crucial role in protecting the northern frontier of the country and were appointed by the reigning king or queen.

The prisoners' carvings are thought to date back to the late 15th century, when the future King Richard III, the Yorkist Richard of Gloucester, was a warden of the castle. The prisoners would while away the time by scratching into the red sandstone, probably with a small nail. Among the carvings are St George killing a dragon, a white boar (the

Carlisle Cathedral is reputedly the second smallest Cathedral in Britain.

personal motif of Richard III), a stag's head, two leaping dolphins and a feathered griffin (all Dacre badges).

There is also a depiction of the crucifixion, with the Virgin Mary and Mary Magdalene in prayer at the foot of the cross.

Carlisle Cathedral

The most remarkable thing about Carlisle Cathedral is that it is still standing. It has been almost ripped to pieces since it was first founded in 1133 and is now much smaller than it was, with many of its stones having being used to patch up the city walls during the Civil War. Nevertheless, it has retained many of its glories, including the magnificent east window with its 14th-century glass.

During its time it has been a witness to great drama. Robert the Bruce had to swear an oath of allegiance to Edward I and was later excommunicated here. The same king, dying on his way to Scotland, dedicated his litter in front of the high altar before starting his last journey to the Solway. After the 1745 rebellion the castle was overflowing, and many Jacobite soldiers were imprisoned in the nave and the bells which had welcomed Prince Charlie were silenced, not to be rung again until 1926. Sir Walter Scott was married here and in 1978 Queen Elizabeth II distributed the Royal Maundy to the citizens.

The building itself could tell almost the whole story of the city. Carlisle has been an important Christian centre since the time of St Cuthbert, who visited in AD686, and a

The Brougham Tryptych, Carlisle Cathedral.

number of eighth to 10th-century crosses have been found in the vicinity, adding weight to the theory that there was a church or monastery on or near the present site.

The cathedral is therefore literally sitting on history. In 1953 Mr G.F. Simpson, an archaeological advisor to the council and a leading authority on the Roman occupation of the north of England, was given permission to dig in the cathedral close. His hole was only eight feet square but its cross section was an astonishing visual record. There is only about half of the Norman cathedral on view now, but he revealed the foundations of the other half and under the foundations he found something else: a huge mass of bones and skulls. An enormous number of bodies had been thrown into a pit, certainly not a Christian burial, but possibly a rearrangement of an existing graveyard to make room for new corpses. That was one theory, but others were also considered.

There could have been a plague or even a massacre. It is in the record books that Halfden the Dane sacked the city in AD875, killing every living thing. Digging deeper, between 14 and 20 feet down Simpson found timber and stonework representing three distinct periods of Roman history.

It was on this site that in 1122, King Henry II founded the Augustinian priory of St Mary. The priory then became the cathedral of the new Diocese of Carlisle and Athelwold of Nostell in Yorkshire became its first bishop; it has been a place of daily Christian worship ever since.

What can be seen today is really only the head and shoulders of the original building: the choir, transepts and the remaining bays of the nave, which was once 140 feet or more of solid Norman arches. From outside the grey Norman stones can clearly be seen against the red sandstone of the later additions. It is all a

Opposite: The organ and magnificent ceiling of Carlisle Cathedral.

The Fratry, Carlisle Cathedral.

The Choir Screen, Carlisle Cathedral.

Chapel, Transept and North Aisle Arches, Carlisle Cathedral.

Opposite: Carlisle Cathedral — the different colours of building stone of different periods can be clearly seen.

bit of a hotchpotch but, considering the fires, the Reformation and the Civil War, it is still an impressive sight.

Inside there is a fabulous contrast of darkness and rich colour. There are ancient painted panels of the lives of St Anthony, St Augustine of Hippo and St Cuthbert; tombs, huge flagstones and two beautiful 16th-century rood screens. The canopies in the choir stalls, carved in the time of King Henry IV, are of dark, almost black wood and they depict fabulous beasts from myths and

legends, including an elegant mermaid. The wood above the heads of the singers soars upwards in a Gothic shower of gables, buttresses, steeples, pinnacles and turrets, leading the eye up to another small miracle — the roof. This is a series of dark blue panels,

Right: Gargoyle in memory of PC George Russell, killed in the line of duty in 1965.

Far right: A carving, thought to be of Edward I, Carlisle Cathedral

Carlisle Citadel
was built by order
of Henry VIII.

Carlisle Citadel (Towers) and Statue of Lord Lonsdale

The statue of the Earl of Lonsdale was erected in 1845.

In 1541 King Henry VIII ordered the southern defences of the city to be strengthened with the addition of two large towers. He was worried about European anger at the recent Dissolution of the Monasteries and was taking no chances that the Scots, backed perhaps by Spanish or French forces, would cause trouble on his northern frontier. The towers were replaced in 1810 and for many years housed the law courts. They are now occupied by county council offices. The statue of the Earl of Lonsdale, whose efforts helped in the rebuilding, was erected in 1845.

Carlisle Stanwix

The wooded plateau to the north of the River Eden was the location of the Alia Petriana, a crack unit of the Roman cavalry consisting of 1,000 horse soldiers when at full strength. The spire of St Michael's Church has been built over the centre of the camp and nothing much remains today. 'Ala' means a 'wing', and its usual battle position was to the side so that it could rapidly reinforce weak points in a formation. In AD69 it was mentioned by Tacitus in connection with some rapid strategic manoeuvres in Italy and was assigned to Britain in AD71. It was then moved to Stanwix in AD130 and was stationed there for 30 years.

each with a flaming sun at the centre of its milky way and it was finished in 1851 by Owen Jones, who decorated the Great Exhibition of 1851. When the dean first took a look at it, all he could utter was 'Oh my stars!' Such is its reputation that the cathedral now receives almost 200,000 visitors a year.

In February 1965 a local policeman called George Russell was shot and killed at Oxenholme railway station when trying to arrest an armed robber travelling south from Scotland. The gargoyle next to him is of the sculptor himself and it is thought to be the only one in the UK wearing glasses.

The grey section of the original Norman transept and nave, built in the 12th century with stones taken from the Roman wall, can clearly be seen next to the red sandstone of the later additions to the cathedral.

It was unusual for such a large force to be concentrated in one spot and it is perhaps an indication of the pivotal importance of Carlisle in the defence of the province. It is likely that it was used as a highly mobile force

Opposite: The Reivers Curse Stone – Carlisle.

capable of rushing to danger points along the Roman wall and to other threatened areas. The unit certainly gained the respect of the Emperor Augustus, who twice awarded honours to it in the shape of a 'torque' for gallantry and its troopers were given automatic citizenship of Rome.

Some Arthurian scholars suggest its reputation for lightning speed and deadly effect gives credence to the legend of King Arthur and his knights. If the legends are to be believed, one of Arthur's advantages in his battles with the Saxons from the east and the Picts from the north was his knowledge of the Roman roads, which were still intact, and the swift marshalling of his cavalry along them. There is still a long tradition in the Borders today, almost unique in Britain, of the Common Ridings, where large bands of mounted men and women ride the boundaries of their territories each year.

Stanwix Roman Cavalry Fort overlooked the River Eden.

The Cursing Stone

The highly-controversial 'cursing stone' was installed outside Tullie House museum in 2001. It's a 14-ton block of granite with a 16th-century curse inscribed on it, which was aimed at Reiver families notorious for terrorising the area. It was a locally inspired attempt at mass excommunication and was read out by priests in every parish.

It is doubtful if the reading had any effect. A travelling clergyman had once asked a group of Borderers if there were any Christians among them and received the answer 'Na, we're a' Elliotts and Armstrongs here...'

Nevertheless, it is a formidable and chilling invective and runs to over 1,500 words. The controversy arose when misfortune began to plague the city shortly after its installation. There were Biblical floods, closures of factories, a murder in a local bakery, an outbreak of foot and mouth disease and Carlisle United were relegated... It was all too much for some local worthies and the removal of the stone was discussed at council level.

The stone is still there and the council pointed out that local Christian groups had literally given a blessing to it and that anyway, it would cost thousands of pounds to remove it. At one point the artist himself, Gordon Young, locally born and a descendant of a Reiver family, joined in the row. He compared the plan to destroy it to the destruction of the giant Buddhas by the Taliban in Afghanistan in 2001. He argued that the stone had nothing to do with the occult and added that if he thought it would affect Carlisle United's performances he would have smashed it himself...

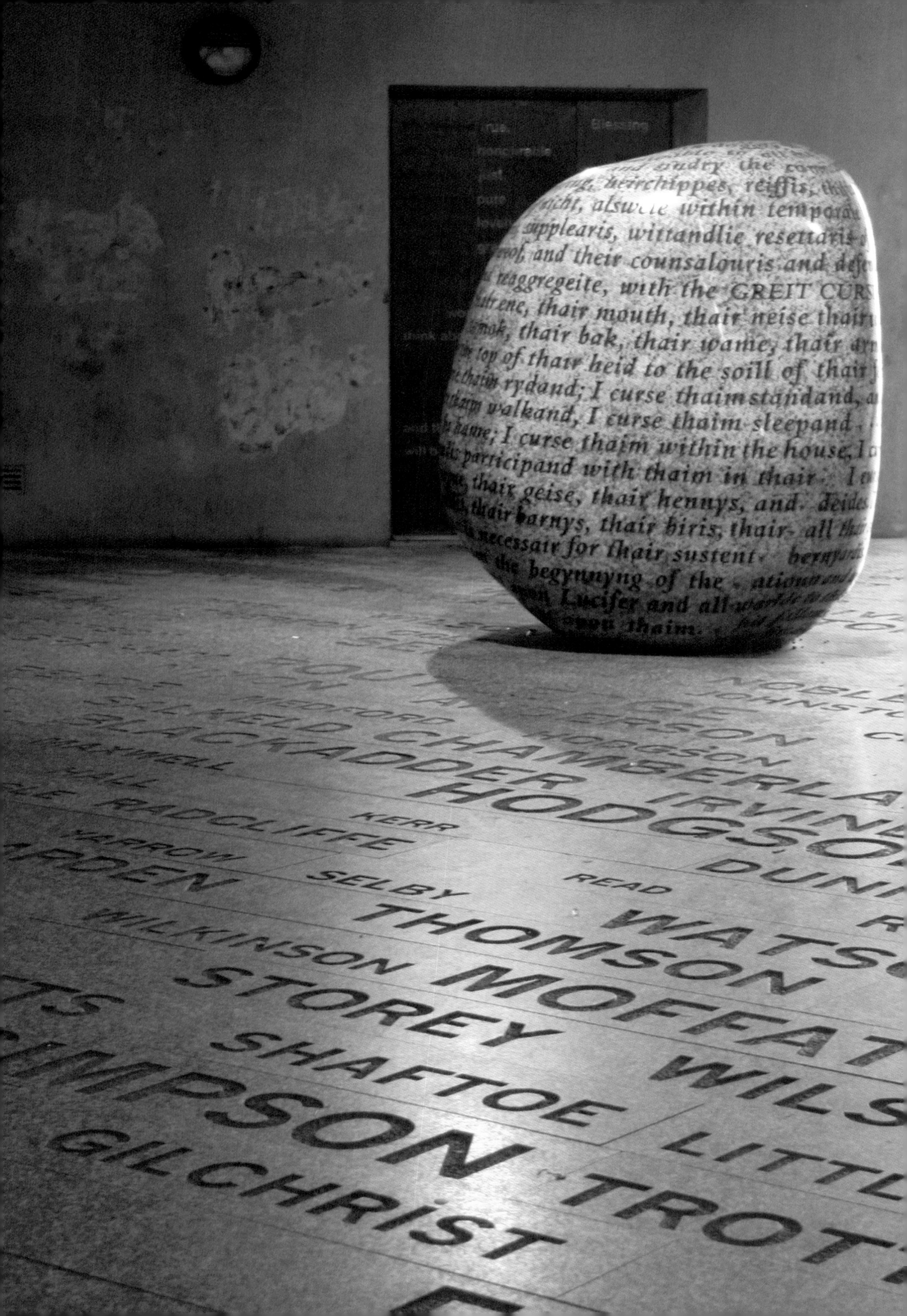

The Turf Tavern was once the grandstand of the old Carlisle Racecourse.

The Turf Tavern, Carlisle

The Turf Tavern is a Grade II listed building. It was built as the grandstand of old Carlisle Race Course between 1839 and 1840. The city has a history of horse racing dating back over 500 years to the days of the Border Reivers. It was, of course, illegal to buy and sell horses across the Border and the only way to have a

look at any potential purchase without incurring the wrath of the law and severe penalty was at a race meeting. Even the wardens showed off their animals to potential buyers under the cover of an organised race meeting.

The West Walls

All that remains of the walls which once protected Carlisle on all sides is the section opposite the cathedral called 'West Walls'.

Built in the 12th century, the walls were once a formidable obstacle and were able to help the city withstand lengthy sieges. In the mediaval period they joined with the castle to form a continuous barrier. Over the centuries there were many harrowing scenes, mainly involving Scottish armies trying to wrest the city back to its former status as the capital of Scotland.

During the Civil War the city was loyal to King Charles I and the Scottish and Parliamentary forces were never able to breach the defences, though the citizens were reduced to eating horseflesh and 'linseed bread' and it became difficult for them to hide the fact that they were starving. In 1645 Parliamentary troops entered the city and one prominent citizen, Isaac Tullie, 'a judicious and observant person' and 'a mortal hater of Roundheads and Scots', kept a journal of the times. The nearby Tullie House is named after him. One of the reasons that Carlisle Cathedral is the shortest in the country is that many of its stones went into repairing and strengthening the walls during this period.

A century later, in 1745, Prince Charles Edward Stuart was proclaimed rightful king of England and Scotland at Carlisle Cross, but this time the citizens decided to stay out of the fight and did not support him as he marched south with his Highland army. He returned a few weeks later with his cousin the Duke of Cumberland snapping at his heels. He left behind him a doomed group of men called the Manchester Regiment to defend the city, but they quickly surrendered when Cumberland's cannon began to blast holes in the castle walls.

Carlisle City Walls date from the 12th century.

Overleaf: The Devorgilla Bridge, Dumfries.

Dumfries

The Midsteeple, Dumfries.

Like many Border towns, Dumfries, sometimes known as 'the Queen of the South', has had a turbulent and eventful history. It is mainly celebrated for its links with the great Robbie Burns, who wrote nearly 100 of his songs while living in the area, but it was also the scene of one of the most dramatic murders in Scotland when Robert the Bruce killed his main rival for the throne.

A church dedicated to St Michael was established at Dumfries during the seventh and eighth century, but it was first founded as a royal burgh in 1186 on the east side of the lowest crossing point of the River Nith. It quickly grew into a market town and port, boasting one of the oldest bridges in the country – named after Lady Devorgilla, the mother of King John Balliol, and built in 1432, 142 years after her death. The bridge has been rebuilt more than once but is still in use today, forming a magnificent backdrop to the Cauld, a foaming weir on the river just below.

Lady Devorgilla was a great heiress at the time and endowed various monasteries along the Solway. At the age of 15 she married John Balliol of Barnard Castle in Yorkshire and when he died she founded Balliol College in Oxford. She is buried in New or Sweetheart Abbey a few miles to the west, with the embalmed heart of her beloved husband clasped to her breast. Another ancient ruin is Lincluden College on the outskirts of the town. It is the remains of a 12th-century Benedictine nunnery, which became a 15th-century collegiate church.

Dumfries was the first port of call for invading armies from England and the town was plundered and sacked on numerous occasions, particularly in 1300, 1448, 1536, 1542, 1547 and 1570. It also suffered during the Civil Wars in the 1640s. The origins of these clashes can probably be traced back to Edward I of England, but it would be unfair to blame him for everything. As a town situated on the fault line between two warring and quarrelsome nations, Dumfries, like Carlisle, was always going to be caught up in any conflict.

The internal power struggle in Scotland really began in Dumfries in February 1306, when Robert the Bruce killed John III Comyn, 'the Red Comyn', before the altar in the church of the now-vanished Greyfriar's Monastery. Comyn was the nephew of John De Balliol, Edward's puppet on the Scottish throne, and his murder precipitated the Scottish Wars of Independence that climaxed in the Scottish victory at Bannockburn in 1314. Edward had Bruce excommunicated,

The plaque marks the place – Old Greyfriars Church – where Robert the Bruce murdered the Red Comyn in 1306.

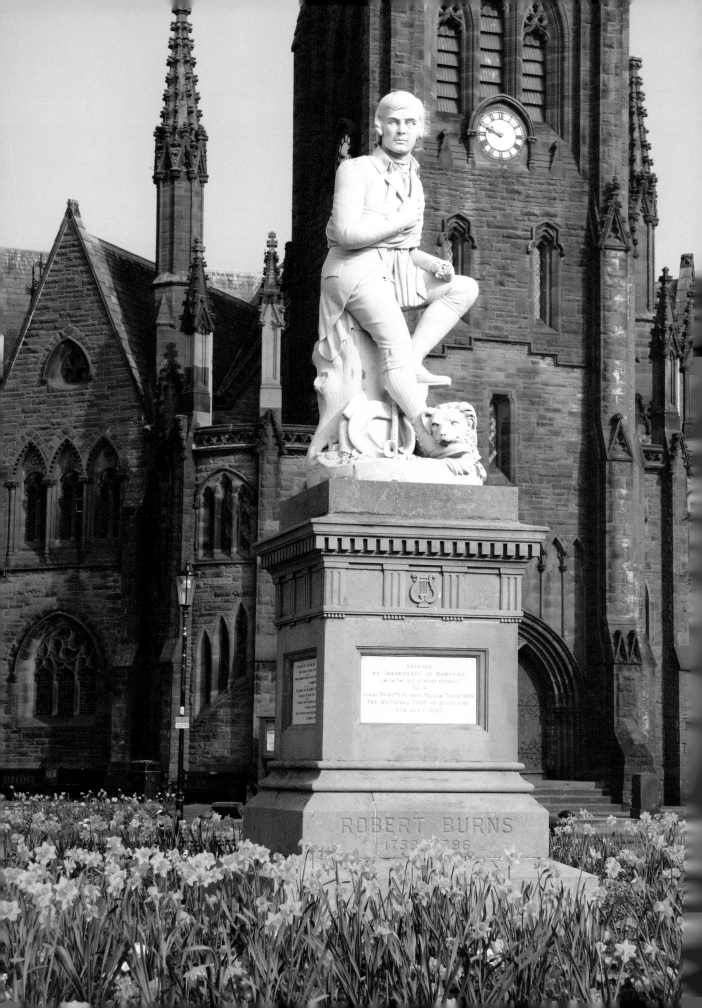

ERECTED
BY INHABITANTS OF DUMFRIES,
(WITH THE AID OF MANY FRIENDS)
AS A
LOVING TRIBUTE TO THEIR FELLOW TOWNSMAN,
THE NATIONAL POET OF SCOTLAND.
6TH APRIL 1882.

ROBERT BURNS
1759   1796

less for the actual murder than for the fact that it was committed in a church, but this didn't stop Bruce progressing to the kingship of Scotland. Greyfriars Church, built in 1868, overlooks the site of the murder on the opposite side of Castle Street, marked by a plaque on a shop wall.

Another prominent landmark is the Midsteeple in the High Street. It was built in the early 17th century as a civic centre and town jail, and a nearby hotel has a Prince Charlie's room where the Young Pretender had his headquarters when he stayed in the town after his retreat from Derby in 1746.

The town was not sympathetic to the Stuart cause and had been pro-Government in both his rising and the previous one of 1715, so the prince decided to impose a large fine and a demand for a thousand pairs of shoes for his Highland army. The citizens knew, though, that the Duke of Cumberland was giving chase and that Charles was a man in a hurry. They haggled and blustered and got away with paying less than half the money and producing considerably fewer shoes, for which they were later reimbursed by the Government. They were under considerable threat, though, and Walter Scott described how the six-year-old daughter of the provost was carried by a Highlander out of her house just before it was to be burned to the ground.

The main boast of the town, however, is its links with Robbie Burns, Scotland's greatest and most-loved poet. He farmed at Ellisland, a few miles up the Nith, and it was here that he composed *Auld Lang Syne*, *To Mary in Heaven* and *Tam o' Shanter*, among many

Opposite: The Statue of Robert Burns, Dumfries.

Robert Burns' House, Dumfries.

The Robert Burns Centre, Dumfries.

The Hole I' the Wall Inn, Dumfries.

Plaque of Burns' poetry - The Hole I' the Wall Inn, Dumfries.

other songs. He wrote *Tam o' Shanter* in one day. He was seen by his wife walking for hours on the banks of the River Nith, swinging his arms to and fro in great excitement. She took the children out to see him but he was in such a trance that he hardly noticed them and continued to walk and recite. She recalls 'I stepped aside with the bairns among the broom, and past us he came, his brow flushed, and his yes shinin'. I wish you could have seen him; he was in such ecstasy that the tears were happin' down his cheeks.'

The poem was such a success that a Professor Wilson later visited the spot and rolled himself on the riverbank, explaining that it was worthwhile trying to catch any remains of genius and humour that Burns might have left there, and the late Alexander Smith thought that the poem was 'the best day's work done in Scotland since the victory of Bruce at Bannockburn'.

Despite his growing fame, Burns was struggling to make a living as a farmer as the soil at Ellisland was so poor, and he moved into Dumfries, concentrating on his job as an exciseman. A highly-sociable and gregarious man, he sadly suffered from poverty in his final years when ill health overcame him and he had to give up his job. Even so, more of his most famous songs such as *Scots wha hae*, *John Anderson* and *My love is like a red, red rose* were written here. There is a fine statue of him in the town centre and his house and favourite pubs, the Globe Inn and the Hole i' the Wa', are now much visited, as is his house in Mill Street (now Burns Street). This has been a place of pilgrimage ever since his death, and early visitors were Dorothy and William Wordsworth, who arrived in

The Burns Mausoleum — St Michael's Church, Dumfries.

Jean Arthur — Robbie Burns' wife.

JEAN ARMOUR
1765 - 1834
WIFE OF ROBERT BURNS
ERECTED BY
BURNS HOWFF CLUB
SEPTEMBER 2004

Dumfries in August 1803. Dorothy described the visit:

'Mrs Burns was gone to spend some time by the sea-shore with her children. We spoke to the servant-maid at the door, who invited us forward, and we sate at the parlour. The walls were coloured with a blue wash; on one side of the fire was a mahogany desk, opposite to the window a clock, and over the desk a print from the "Cotter's Saturday Night", which Burns mentions in one of his letters having received as a present. The house was cleanly and neat in the inside, the stairs of stone, scoured white, the kitchen on the right side of the passage, the parlour on the left. In the room above the parlour, the Poet died…'

According to some of the more sanctimonious 19th-century biographers, it was the demon drink that hastened his end. It is probably true to say, though that Burns drank no more than his friends and that his death was caused by heart failure, brought on by the stresses and strains put on his body by the harsh ploughing life at his father's Ayrshire farm when he was a young man. His legacy is undiminished and he is now celebrated worldwide as the champion of brotherhood and the common man. Apart from his great patriotic song *Scots wha hae wi' Wallace bled*, his incomparable *A man's a man for a' that* reaffirms that the noblest work of God is the dignity and independence of the honest toiler:

'The Honest man though e'er sae poor, is king of men for a' that.'

A less famous author, J.M. Barrie, author of *Peter Pan*, was a pupil at Dumfries Academy, as was John Laurie, who played Fraser in *Dad's Army*.

One of the strangest things to happen in Dumfries was a riot that took place on 6 February 1829. Burke and Hare, the notorious bodysnatchers who plied their grisly trade in Edinburgh, had spread fear and loathing throughout the length and breadth of Scotland. Burke had been tried and executed but Hare escaped the gallows by turning King's evidence. He was granted safe passage home to Ireland and on the way to the port the coach stopped over in Dumfries. The news soon spread and a seething mob of over 1,000 people gathered outside the Kings Arms Hotel where he was staying, intent on doing him harm — a gang broke down the door and tried to kill him but he was bundled upstairs to the safety of an attic room. The coach was due to leave at 11am but Hare thought it was too dangerous to board and it left without him. The mob followed it to the top of Buccleuch Street where they stopped and pulled open the doors... no Hare!... the mob surged back to the hotel, braying for his life.

A furious woman tried to strangle him in front of the police officers protecting him! Things were rapidly coming to a head and he was eventually smuggled out. The police set up a decoy and took him, under cover, to the local prison for his own safety. But the howling mob still persevered; they tried to burn down the building and over 100 special constables had to be brought in as reinforcements. Eventually Hare resumed his journey — but he had to change his route and travel a circuitous route through England to made good his escape.

Six months later his sister arrived in Dumfries to collect some clothes he had left in his hurry to get away. They were pointed out to her, still in a heap in the corner of the attic — no one would go near them.